Learn Korean Language Mastery: Level 1 For Beginners –

Easy Learning In Your Car Or While Sleeping!

By Jiho Park

Free PDF Download Included!

Table Of Contents

Language Learning Tips

Embarking on a journey to learn a new language can be an exhilarating yet challenging experience. For English speakers delving into the world of Korean, the task may seem daunting due to linguistic differences and unfamiliar writing systems. However, with the right strategies and dedication, mastering Korean is not only achievable but also immensely rewarding. In this comprehensive guide, we will explore various language learning tips tailored specifically for English speakers aiming to learn Korean.

Understanding the Language Structure:

Grasp the Alphabet (Hangul): One of the initial hurdles in learning Korean is adapting to the Hangul writing system. Unlike the Roman alphabet, Hangul consists of characters representing both consonants and vowels, organized into syllabic blocks. Dedicate time to familiarize yourself with these characters, their pronunciation, and the combinations that form syllables. Online resources, apps, and flashcards can be invaluable tools for this purpose.

Focus on Pronunciation: Korean pronunciation is crucial for effective communication. Pay attention to subtle nuances in sounds that may not exist in English. Practice listening to native speakers through language apps, dramas, or music to develop an ear for the language. Mimicking native pronunciation can enhance your speaking skills and make interactions more natural.

Building a Strong Foundation:

Start with Basic Vocabulary: Begin your Korean language journey by learning essential vocabulary and common phrases. Focus on everyday words, greetings, and basic conversational elements. Utilize language learning apps, textbooks, and online resources to build a foundational vocabulary that you can expand upon as you progress.

Master Common Phrases: Memorize and practice common Korean phrases used in daily life. This not only aids in practical communication but also helps in understanding sentence structure and word order.

Learn Basic Grammar: Understanding the fundamental grammatical structures of Korean is essential for constructing coherent sentences. Start with basic sentence patterns, verb conjugations, and sentence endings.

Developing Language Skills:

Immerse Yourself in Korean Media: Exposure to authentic Korean content is an excellent way to enhance language skills. Watch Korean dramas, movies, variety shows, and listen to K-pop music. This immersion not only aids in improving listening skills but also introduces colloquial expressions and cultural nuances.

Read Korean Texts: Gradually progress to reading Korean texts such as simple articles, children's books, or webtoons. This practice enhances reading comprehension, expands vocabulary, and exposes you to different writing styles. Don't shy away from using online dictionaries to aid in understanding unfamiliar words and expressions.

Write Regularly: Develop your writing skills by keeping a language journal, writing short essays, or engaging in online forums in Korean. This not only reinforces vocabulary and grammar but also builds confidence in expressing yourself in the language.

Cultural Understanding:

Learn About Korean Culture: Language and culture are intricately connected. Enhance your language learning journey by delving into Korean culture, customs, and traditions. Understanding the cultural context behind certain expressions or social norms will deepen your appreciation for the language.

Participate in Language Exchange Events: Attend language exchange events or cultural gatherings to connect with native Korean speakers. These interactions provide real-world applications of the language and opportunities to make friends who can guide you through the intricacies of Korean culture.

Overcoming Challenges:

Stay Persistent and Patient: Language learning is a gradual process that requires persistence and patience. Set realistic goals, celebrate small victories, and acknowledge that making mistakes is a natural part of the learning journey. Consistency and dedication will ultimately lead to significant progress.

Seek Feedback: Actively seek feedback on your language skills. Whether from language exchange partners, teachers, or online communities, constructive criticism can help identify areas for improvement and guide your focus in the learning process.

Join Language Learning Communities: Connect with fellow Korean learners through online forums, social media groups, or local language meet-ups. Sharing experiences, asking questions, and supporting each other creates a sense of community that can be motivating and beneficial for your language learning journey.

Conclusion:

Embarking on the adventure of learning Korean as an English speaker is a challenging yet rewarding endeavor. By mastering the Hangul alphabet, building a strong foundation in vocabulary and grammar, and immersing yourself in Korean culture, you can overcome the initial hurdles and make steady progress. Consistent practice, exposure to authentic content, and a positive mindset are key elements in achieving language proficiency. Embrace the journey, stay committed, and enjoy the process of unlocking the beauty of the Korean language and culture.

Essential Expressions:

Hello. - 안녕하세요. (Annyeonghaseyo.)

Hello. - 안녕하세요. (Annyeonghaseyo.)

Hi. - 안녕. (Annyeong.)

Hi. - 안녕. (Annyeong.)

Good morning. - 좋은 아침이에요. (Joeun achimi-e-yo.)

Good morning. - 좋은 아침이에요. (Joeun achimi-e-yo.)

Good afternoon. - 좋은 오후에요. (Joeun ohu-e-yo.)

Good afternoon. - 좋은 오후에요. (Joeun ohu-e-yo.)

Good evening. - 좋은 저녁이에요. (Joeun jeonyeok-i-e-yo.)

Good evening. - 좋은 저녁이에요. (Joeun jeonyeok-i-e-yo.)

Good night. - 안녕히 주무세요. (Annyeonghi jumuseyo.)

Good night. - 안녕히 주무세요. (Annyeonghi jumuseyo.)

How are you? - 어떻게 지내세요? (Eotteoke jinaeseyo?)

How are you? - 어떻게 지내세요? (Eotteoke jinaeseyo?)

I'm fine, thank you. - 잘 지냈어요, 감사합니다. (Jal jinaesseoyo, gamsahamnida.)

I'm fine, thank you. - 잘 지냈어요, 감사합니다. (Jal jinaesseoyo, gamsahamnida.)

What's your name? - 이름이 뭐에요? (Ireumi mwoeyo?)

What's your name? - 이름이 뭐에요? (Ireumi mwoeyo?)

My name is [your name]. - 제 이름은 [your name]이에요. (Je ireumeun [your name]-i-e-yo.)

My name is [your name]. - 제 이름은 [your name]이에요. (Je ireumeun [your name]-i-e-yo.)

Please. - 제발. (Jebal.)

Please. - 제발. (Jebal.)

Thank you. - 감사합니다. (Gamsahamnida.)

Thank you. - 감사합니다. (Gamsahamnida.)

Sorry. - 미안해요. (Mianhaeyo.)

Sorry. - 미안해요. (Mianhaeyo.)

Excuse me. - 실례합니다. (Sillyehamnida.)

Excuse me. - 실례합니다. (Sillyehamnida.)

You're welcome. - 천만에요. (Cheonmaneyo.)

You're welcome. - 천만에요. (Cheonmaneyo.)

Yes. - 네. (Ne.)

Yes. - 네. (Ne.)

No. - 아니요. (Aniyo.)

No. - 아니요. (Aniyo.)

Maybe. - 아마도. (Amado.)

Maybe. - 아마도. (Amado.)

I don't know. - 잘 모르겠어요. (Jal moreugesseoyo.)

I don't know. - 잘 모르겠어요. (Jal moreugesseoyo.)

I understand. - 이해해요. (Ihaehaeyo.)

I understand. - 이해해요. (Ihaehaeyo.)

Thank you very much. - 정말 감사합니다.
(Jeongmal gamsahamnida.)

Thank you very much. - 정말 감사합니다.
(Jeongmal gamsahamnida.)

I appreciate it. - 감사해요. (Gamsa haeyo.)

I appreciate it. - 감사해요. (Gamsa haeyo.)

I'm sorry. - 미안해요. (Mianhaeyo.)

I'm sorry. - 미안해요. (Mianhaeyo.)

I apologize. - 사과합니다. (Sagwahamnida.)

I apologize. - 사과합니다. (Sagwahamnida.)

It's okay. - 괜찮아요. (Gwaenchanayo.)

It's okay. - 괜찮아요. (Gwaenchanayo.)

No problem. - 문제 없어요. (Munje eopseoyo.)

No problem. - 문제 없어요. (Munje eopseoyo.)

Please forgive me. - 용서해주세요. (Yongseohae juseyo.)

Please forgive me. - 용서해주세요. (Yongseohae juseyo.)

Excuse my mistake. - 실수로 인해 죄송합니다. (Silsuro inhae joesonghamnida.)

Excuse my mistake. - 실수로 인해 죄송합니다. (Silsuro inhae joesonghamnida.)

Thanks for your help. - 도움 주셔서 감사합니다. (Doum jusyeoseo gamsahamnida.)

Thanks for your help. - 도움 주셔서 감사합니다. (Doum jusyeoseo gamsahamnida.)

I owe you one. - 신세를 지고 있어요. (Sinseleul jigo isseoyo.)

I owe you one. - 신세를 지고 있어요. (Sinseleul jigo isseoyo.)

Nice to meet you. - 만나서 반갑습니다. (Mannaseo bangapseumnida.)

Nice to meet you. - 만나서 반갑습니다. (Mannaseo bangapseumnida.)

Have a nice day. - 좋은 하루 되세요. (Joeun haru doeseyo.)

Have a nice day. - 좋은 하루 되세요. (Joeun haru doeseyo.)

Good luck! - 행운을 빕니다! (Haeng-un-eul bibnida!)

Good luck! - 행운을 빕니다! (Haeng-un-eul bibnida!)

Congratulations! - 축하합니다! (Chukha hamnida!)

Congratulations! - 축하합니다! (Chukha hamnida!)

What's up? - 어떻게 지내? (Eotteoke jinae?)

What's up? - 어떻게 지내? (Eotteoke jinae?)

Long time no see. - 오랜만이에요. (Oraenmani-e-yo.)

Long time no see. - 오랜만이에요. (Oraenmani-e-yo.)

Take care. - 건강하세요. (Geonganghaseyo.)

Take care. - 건강하세요. (Geonganghaseyo.)

I miss you. - 보고 싶어요. (Bogo sip-eoyo.)

I miss you. - 보고 싶어요. (Bogo sip-eoyo.)

I love you. - 사랑해요. (Salanghaeyo.)

I love you. - 사랑해요. (Salanghaeyo.)

Goodbye. - 안녕히 가세요. (Annyeonghi gaseyo.)

Goodbye. - 안녕히 가세요. (Annyeonghi gaseyo.)

Where are you from? - 어디서 오셨어요? (Eodiseo osyeosseoyo?)

Where are you from? - 어디서 오셨어요? (Eodiseo osyeosseoyo?)

What do you do? - 무슨 일 하세요? (Museun il haseyo?)

What do you do? - 무슨 일 하세요? (Museun il haseyo?)

How was your day? - 하루 어땠어요? (Haru eottae-seo-yo?)

How was your day? - 하루 어땠어요? (Haru eottae-seo-yo?)

Can I help you? - 도와드릴까요? (Dowadeurilkkayo?)

Can I help you? - 도와드릴까요? (Dowadeurilkkayo?)

What time is it? - 지금 몇 시에요? (Jigeum myeot shi-e-yo?)

What time is it? - 지금 몇 시에요? (Jigeum myeot shi-e-yo?)

May I have the bill, please? - 계산서 주세요. (Gyesanseo juseyo.)

May I have the bill, please? - 계산서 주세요. (Gyesanseo juseyo.)

I don't understand. - 이해하지 못해요. (Ihaehaji mothaeyo.)

I don't understand. - 이해하지 못해요. (Ihaehaji mothaeyo.)

Can you repeat that? - 그 말을 다시 해 주세요. (Geu mareul dasi hae juseyo.)

Can you repeat that? - 그 말을 다시 해 주세요. (Geu mareul dasi hae juseyo.)

Where is the restroom? - 화장실 어디에요? (Hwajangsil eodi-e-yo?)

Where is the restroom? - 화장실 어디에요? (Hwajangsil eodi-e-yo?)

What's the weather like today? - 오늘 날씨 어때요? (Oneul nalssi eottaeyo?)

What's the weather like today? - 오늘 날씨 어때요? (Oneul nalssi eottaeyo?)

What's the plan for today? - 오늘 일정이 어때요? (Oneul iljeong-i eottaeyo?)

What's the plan for today? - 오늘 일정이 어때요? (Oneul iljeong-i eottaeyo?)

Can I get your opinion on something? - 한 번 물어볼게요. (Han beon muleobolgeyo.)

Can I get your opinion on something? - 한 번 물어볼게요. (Han beon muleobolgeyo.)

That's interesting! - 흥미로워요! (Heungmilowoyo!)

That's interesting! - 흥미로워요! (Heungmilowoyo!)

I have a question. - 질문이 있어요. (Jilmun-i iss-eoyo.)

I have a question. - 질문이 있어요. (Jilmun-i iss-eoyo.)

Let's hang out sometime. - 언젠가 같이 놀아요. (Eonjenga gat-i nol-ayo.)

Let's hang out sometime. - 언젠가 같이 놀아요. (Eonjenga gat-i nol-ayo.)

What do you enjoy doing in your free time? - 여가 시간에 뭐 하세요? (Yeoga sigane mwo haseyo?)

What do you enjoy doing in your free time? - 여가 시간에 뭐 하세요? (Yeoga sigane mwo haseyo?)

I can't believe it! - 믿을 수 없어요! (Mideul su eobs-eoyo!)

I can't believe it! - 믿을 수 없어요! (Mideul su eobs-eoyo!)

Don't worry, everything will be okay. - 걱정 마세요, 모든 게 괜찮을 거에요. (Geogjeong maseyo, modeun ge gwaenchanh-eul geoeyo.)

Don't worry, everything will be okay. - 걱정 마세요, 모든 게 괜찮을 거에요. (Geogjeong maseyo, modeun ge gwaenchanh-eul geoeyo.)

I'm looking forward to it. - 기대돼요. (Gidaedwaeyo.)

I'm looking forward to it. - 기대돼요. (Gidaedwaeyo.)

It's a small world! - 세상이 정말 좁아요! (Sesang-i jeongmal jobaoyo!)

It's a small world! - 세상이 정말 좁아요! (Sesang-i jeongmal jobaoyo!)

Basic Interactions

Do you come here often? - 여기 자주 오시나요? (Yeogi jaju osinayo?)

Do you come here often? - 여기 자주 오시나요? (Yeogi jaju osinayo?)

I'm learning Korean. Can you help me practice? - 저는 한국어를 배우고 있어요. 연습을 좀 도와주실 수 있나요

I'm learning Korean. Can you help me practice? -
저는 한국어를 배우고 있어요. 연습을 좀
도와주실 수 있나요?

What's your favorite Korean food? - 좋아하는 한국
음식이 뭐예요?

What's your favorite Korean food? - 좋아하는 한국
음식이 뭐예요

Have you seen any good movies lately? -최근에 본
좋은 영화 있나요?

 Have you seen any good movies lately? -최근에 본
좋은 영화 있나요?

Can you recommend a nice place to visit around
here? -여기 근처에 가볼 만한 좋은 곳 추천해 줄
수 있나요?

Can you recommend a nice place to visit around
here? -여기 근처에 가볼 만한 좋은 곳 추천해 줄
수 있나요?

How do you like to spend your weekends? 주말에
뭐 하는 걸 좋아하나요?

How do you like to spend your weekends? 주말에
뭐 하는 걸 좋아하나요?

What kind of music do you listen to? 어떤 종류의
음악을 듣나요?

What kind of music do you listen to? 어떤 종류의
음악을 듣나요?

Are you interested in sports? - 스포츠에 관심 있나요?

Are you interested in sports? - 스포츠에 관심 있나요?

What's your favorite part about living in Korea? - 한국에서 살면서 가장 좋아하는 점이 무엇인가요?

What's your favorite part about living in Korea? - 한국에서 살면서 가장 좋아하는 점이 무엇인가요?

Do you enjoy traveling within Korea? - 한국 내에서 여행하는 것을 즐기나요?

Do you enjoy traveling within Korea? - 한국 내에서 여행하는 것을 즐기나요?

Hope to see you again soon! - 곧 다시 뵙기를 바랍니다!

Hope to see you again soon! - 곧 다시 뵙기를 바랍니다!

It was great talking to you. - 당신과 대화하는 것이 좋았어요.

It was great talking to you. - 당신과 대화하는 것이 좋았어요.

Stay in touch! - 연락 계속 하세요!

Stay in touch! - 연락 계속 하세요!

Wishing you all the best. -모든 것이 잘 되기를 바랍니다.

Wishing you all the best. -모든 것이 잘 되기를 바랍니다.

Let's plan to meet again.- 다시 만날 계획을 세웁시다.

Let's plan to meet again.- 다시 만날 계획을 세웁시다.

Safe travels back home. - 집에 돌아가실 때 안전한 여행 되세요.

Safe travels back home. - 집에 돌아가실 때 안전한 여행 되세요.

Good luck with everything. - 모든 일에 행운을 빕니다.

Good luck with everything. - 모든 일에 행운을 빕니다.

Remember to visit us again! - 다시 우리를 방문해 주세요!

Remember to visit us again! - 다시 우리를 방문해 주세요!

It was a pleasure to meet you. - 당신을 만나게 되어 기뻤습니다.

It was a pleasure to meet you. - 당신을 만나게 되어 기뻤습니다.

Have a wonderful day ahead! - 앞으로 멋진 하루 되세요!

Have a wonderful day ahead! - 앞으로 멋진 하루 되세요!

Asking for Recommendations:

Where can I listen to live traditional Korean music? - 전통 한국 음악을 생생하게 들을 수 있는 곳이 어디인가요?

Where can I listen to live traditional Korean music? - 전통 한국 음악을 생생하게 들을 수 있는 곳이 어디인가요?

I'm looking for a tranquil spot to experience the local nature. Any suggestions?- 현지 자연을 경험할 수 있는 조용한 장소를 찾고 있어요. 추천해 줄 수 있나요?

I'm looking for a tranquil spot to experience the local nature. Any suggestions?- 현지 자연을 경험할 수 있는 조용한 장소를 찾고 있어요. 추천해 줄 수 있나요?

Are there any artisan workshops or markets where I can see crafts being made? - 공예품이 만들어지는 것을 볼 수 있는 장인 워크숍이나 시장이 있나요?

Are there any artisan workshops or markets where I can see crafts being made? - 공예품이 만들어지는 것을 볼 수 있는 장인 워크숍이나 시장이 있나요?

What's a local delicacy that most tourists don't know about? - 대부분의 관광객들이 모르는 현지 별미가 무엇인가요?

What's a local delicacy that most tourists don't know about? - 대부분의 관광객들이 모르는 현지 별미가 무엇인가요?

Can you point me to a neighborhood that's perfect for a leisurely stroll? - 여유롭게 산책하기 좋은 동네를 알려줄 수 있나요?

Can you point me to a neighborhood that's perfect for a leisurely stroll? - 여유롭게 산책하기 좋은 동네를 알려줄 수 있나요?

What's a hidden gem in this area that I shouldn't miss? - 이 지역에서 놓치지 말아야 할 숨겨진 보석 같은 곳이 있나요?

What's a hidden gem in this area that I shouldn't miss? - 이 지역에서 놓치지 말아야 할 숨겨진 보석 같은 곳이 있나요?

Is there a local favorite spot you'd recommend for a unique experience? - 독특한 경험을 할 수 있는 현지인이 좋아하는 장소가 있나요?

Is there a local favorite spot you'd recommend for a unique experience? - 독특한 경험을 할 수 있는 현지인이 좋아하는 장소가 있나요?

Where can I find the best local food that's not in the guidebooks? - 가이드북에 없는 최고의 현지 음식을 어디서 찾을 수 있나요?

Where can I find the best local food that's not in the guidebooks? - 가이드북에 없는 최고의 현지 음식을 어디서 찾을 수 있나요?

I love nature. Do you know any secret natural spots around here? - 자연을 좋아해요. 여기 근처에 비밀스러운 자연 명소가 있나요?

I love nature. Do you know any secret natural spots around here? - 자연을 좋아해요. 여기 근처에 비밀스러운 자연 명소가 있나요?

Are there any hidden alleys or streets full of history? - 역사가 가득한 숨겨진 골목이나 거리가 있나요?

Are there any hidden alleys or streets full of history? - 역사가 가득한 숨겨진 골목이나 거리가 있나요?

I'm interested in local art. Any lesser-known galleries or art spaces? - 현지 예술에 관심이 많아요. 덜 알려진 갤러리나 예술 공간이 있나요?

I'm interested in local art. Any lesser-known galleries or art spaces? - 현지 예술에 관심이 많아요. 덜 알려진 갤러리나 예술 공간이 있나요?

Can you suggest a cozy spot for some quiet reading or relaxing? - 조용히 책을 읽거나 휴식을 취할 수 있는 아늑한 장소를 추천해 줄 수 있나요?

Can you suggest a cozy spot for some quiet reading or relaxing? - 조용히 책을 읽거나 휴식을 취할 수 있는 아늑한 장소를 추천해 줄 수 있나요?

Is there an underrated museum or cultural site here that you love? - 여기서 당신이 좋아하는 과소평가된 박물관이나 문화 사이트가 있나요?

Is there an underrated museum or cultural site here that you love? - 여기서 당신이 좋아하는 과소평가된 박물관이나 문화 사이트가 있나요?

What's a great place for photography that only locals know about? - 현지인만 아는 사진 찍기 좋은 장소가 어디인가요?

What's a great place for photography that only locals know about? - 현지인만 아는 사진 찍기 좋은 장소가 어디인가요?

Is there a place here where I can experience something unique to Korean culture? - 한국 문화에 특유한 것을 경험할 수 있는 곳이 여기 있나요?

Is there a place here where I can experience something unique to Korean culture? - 한국 문화에 특유한 것을 경험할 수 있는 곳이 여기 있나요?

Discussion and Heritage

What historical site here tells the most interesting story? - 여기서 가장 흥미로운 이야기를 전하는 역사적인 장소는 어디인가요?

What historical site here tells the most interesting story? - 여기서 가장 흥미로운 이야기를 전하는 역사적인 장소는 어디인가요?

Can you explain the significance of this monument? - 이 기념물의 중요성을 설명해 줄 수 있나요?

Can you explain the significance of this monument? - 이 기념물의 중요성을 설명해 줄 수 있나요?

I'm fascinated by traditional Korean architecture. Where should I start? - 전통 한국 건축에 매료되었어요. 어디서부터 시작해야 하나요?

I'm fascinated by traditional Korean architecture. Where should I start? - 전통 한국 건축에 매료되었어요. 어디서부터 시작해야 하나요?

What's a must-see temple with a rich history? - 역사가 풍부한 반드시 봐야 할 사원이 있나요?

What's a must-see temple with a rich history? - 역사가 풍부한 반드시 봐야 할 사원이 있나요?

Is there a story behind these ancient ruins? - 이 고대 유적에는 어떤 이야기가 있나요?

Is there a story behind these ancient ruins? - 이 고대 유적에는 어떤 이야기가 있나요?

How has this area's history shaped its current culture? - 이 지역의 역사가 현재의 문화를 어떻게 형성했나요?

How has this area's history shaped its current culture? - 이 지역의 역사가 현재의 문화를 어떻게 형성했나요?

Can you recommend a cultural festival that embodies the spirit of this place? - 이곳의 정신을 담은 문화 축제를 추천해 줄 수 있나요?

Can you recommend a cultural festival that embodies the spirit of this place? - 이곳의 정신을 담은 문화 축제를 추천해 줄 수 있나요?

What local legend or folklore is most beloved here? - 여기서 가장 사랑받는 지역 전설이나 민속은 무엇인가요?

What local legend or folklore is most beloved here? - 여기서 가장 사랑받는 지역 전설이나 민속은 무엇인가요?

Where can I learn more about the traditional crafts of this region? - 이 지역의 전통 공예에 대해 더 배울 수 있는 곳은 어디인가요?

Where can I learn more about the traditional crafts of this region? - 이 지역의 전통 공예에 대해 더 배울 수 있는 곳은 어디인가요?

Is there a historical figure from this area whose story you find inspiring? - 이 지역 출신으로, 당신이 영감을 받는 역사적 인물이 있나요?

Is there a historical figure from this area whose story you find inspiring? - 이 지역 출신으로, 당신이 영감을 받는 역사적 인물이 있나요?

What's the oldest building in this town, and what's its story? - 이 마을에서 가장 오래된 건물은 무엇이며, 그 이야기는 무엇인가요?

What's the oldest building in this town, and what's its story? - 이 마을에서 가장 오래된 건물은 무엇이며, 그 이야기는 무엇인가요?

Where can I find a gallery or museum that features work by local artists? - 현지 예술가들의 작품을 볼 수 있는 갤러리나 박물관이 어디 있나요?

Where can I find a gallery or museum that features work by local artists? - 현지 예술가들의 작품을 볼 수 있는 갤러리나 박물관이 어디 있나요?

Is there a significant historical event that occurred in this area? - 이 지역에서 발생한 중요한 역사적 사건이 있나요?

Is there a significant historical event that occurred in this area? - 이 지역에서 발생한 중요한 역사적 사건이 있나요?

Can you tell me about a traditional festival I should experience while I'm here? - 제가 여기 있는 동안 경험해야 할 전통 축제에 대해 알려줄 수 있나요?

Can you tell me about a traditional festival I should experience while I'm here? - 제가 여기 있는 동안 경험해야 할 전통 축제에 대해 알려줄 수 있나요?

What is a piece of local folklore that captures the spirit of this place? - 이 장소의 정신을 포착하는 현지 민속이 있나요?

What is a piece of local folklore that captures the spirit of this place? - 이 장소의 정신을 포착하는 현지 민속이 있나요?

Heartfelt Connections:

You have a wonderful sense of humor that lights up the room. - 방을 밝게 만드는 멋진 유머 감각을 가지고 계세요.

You have a wonderful sense of humor that lights up the room. - 방을 밝게 만드는 멋진 유머 감각을 가지고 계세요.

Your positive energy is truly infectious. It's always a joy to be around you.- 당신의 긍정적인 에너지는 정말 전염됩니다. 항상 당신 주변에 있으면 기쁩니다.

Your positive energy is truly infectious. It's always a joy to be around you.- 당신의 긍정적인 에너지는 정말 전염됩니다. 항상 당신 주변에 있으면 기쁩니다.

The passion you put into your work is admirable. It really shows in the results. - 당신이 일에 쏟는 열정이 존경스러워요. 결과에서 정말 드러납니다.

The passion you put into your work is admirable. It really shows in the results. - 당신이 일에 쏟는 열정이 존경스러워요. 결과에서 정말 드러납니다.

You have such a unique perspective; I learn so much from you.- 정말 독특한 관점을 가지고 계세요; 저는 당신에게서 많이 배웁니다.

You have such a unique perspective; I learn so much from you.- 정말 독특한 관점을 가지고 계세요; 저는 당신에게서 많이 배웁니다.

Your creativity knows no bounds. I'm always amazed by your ideas. - 당신의 창의력에는 한계가 없어요. 항상 당신의 아이디어에 놀랍니다.

Your creativity knows no bounds. I'm always amazed by your ideas. - 당신의 창의력에는 한계가 없어요. 항상 당신의 아이디어에 놀랍니다.

Your positive energy is contagious. It's always a joy to be around you. - 당신의 긍정적인 에너지가 전염됩니다. 당신과 함께 있으면 항상 기쁩니다.

Your positive energy is contagious. It's always a joy to be around you. - 당신의 긍정적인 에너지가 전염됩니다. 당신과 함께 있으면 항상 기쁩니다.

The way you handled that situation was impressive. You have remarkable problem-solving skills. - 그 상황을 처리한 방식이 인상적이었습니다. 당신은 뛰어난 문제 해결 능력을 가지고 있습니다.

The way you handled that situation was impressive. You have remarkable problem-solving skills. - 그 상황을 처리한 방식이 인상적이었습니다. 당신은 뛰어난 문제 해결 능력을 가지고 있습니다.

You have a wonderful sense of humor that lights up the whole room. - 당신은 방 전체를 밝게 하는 멋진 유머 감각을 가지고 있습니다.

You have a wonderful sense of humor that lights up the whole room. - 당신은 방 전체를 밝게 하는 멋진 유머 감각을 가지고 있습니다.

Your creativity knows no bounds. I'm always amazed by your ideas. - 당신의 창의력에는 경계가 없습니다. 당신의 아이디어에 항상 놀랍니다.

Your creativity knows no bounds. I'm always amazed by your ideas. - 당신의 창의력에는 경계가 없습니다. 당신의 아이디어에 항상 놀랍니다.

Expressions of Gratitude:

I appreciate your patience and understanding more than words can express. - 말로 표현할 수 없을 만큼 당신의 인내와 이해에 감사드립니다.

I appreciate your patience and understanding more than words can express. - 말로 표현할 수 없을 만큼 당신의 인내와 이해에 감사드립니다.

Your guidance has been a beacon for me. Thank you for leading the way. - 당신의 지도가 저에게 등대와 같았어요. 길을 인도해 주셔서 감사합니다.

Your guidance has been a beacon for me. Thank you for leading the way. - 당신의 지도가 저에게 등대와 같았어요. 길을 인도해 주셔서 감사합니다.

Thank you for always listening. Your empathy and support are invaluable. - 항상 들어주셔서 감사합니다. 당신의 공감과 지원은 매우 소중합니다.

Thank you for always listening. Your empathy and support are invaluable. - 항상 들어주셔서 감사합니다. 당신의 공감과 지원은 매우 소중합니다.

I'm so thankful for the moments we share. They mean a lot to me. - 우리가 함께하는 순간들에 정말 감사해요. 그것들은 저에게 많은 의미가 있어요.

I'm so thankful for the moments we share. They mean a lot to me. - 우리가 함께하는 순간들에 정말 감사해요. 그것들은 저에게 많은 의미가 있어요.

Your generosity has touched my heart deeply. Thank you from the bottom of my heart. - 당신의 너그러움이 제 마음 깊숙이 감동을 주었습니다. 진심으로 감사드립니다.

Your generosity has touched my heart deeply. Thank you from the bottom of my heart. - 당신의 너그러움이 제 마음 깊숙이 감동을 주었습니다. 진심으로 감사드립니다.

This means so much to me. Your thoughtfulness will always be remembered. - 이것은 저에게 매우 큰 의미입니다. 당신의 사려 깊음은 항상 기억될 것입니다.

This means so much to me. Your thoughtfulness will always be remembered. - 이것은 저에게 매우 큰 의미입니다. 당신의 사려 깊음은 항상 기억될 것입니다.

I appreciate your advice and support more than words can say. - 말로 표현할 수 없을 정도로 당신의 조언과 지원에 감사드립니다.

I appreciate your advice and support more than words can say. - 말로 표현할 수 없을 정도로 당신의 조언과 지원에 감사드립니다.

Thank you for being a light in my life. Your friendship is a gift. - 제 인생의 빛이 되어 주셔서 감사합니다. 당신의 우정은 선물입니다.

Thank you for being a light in my life. Your friendship is a gift. - 제 인생의 빛이 되어 주셔서 감사합니다. 당신의 우정은 선물입니다.

Your generosity has touched my heart. Thank you for being so giving. - 당신의 너그러움이 제 마음을 감동시켰어요. 그렇게 베풀어 주셔서 감사합니다.

Your generosity has touched my heart. Thank you for being so giving. - 당신의 너그러움이 제 마음을 감동시켰어요. 그렇게 베풀어 주셔서 감사합니다.

Retail Therapy

Could you offer a special price if I buy two? - 두 개를 사면 특별 가격을 제공할 수 있나요?

Could you offer a special price if I buy two? - 두 개를 사면 특별 가격을 제공할 수 있나요?

This is beautiful, but a bit out of my budget. Can we meet in the middle? - 이건 정말 아름답지만, 제 예산을 조금 넘어가요. 가격을 조정할 수 있나요?

This is beautiful, but a bit out of my budget. Can we meet in the middle? - 이건 정말 아름답지만, 제 예산을 조금 넘어가요. 가격을 조정할 수 있나요?

Is there a discount for first-time customers? - 첫 구매 고객을 위한 할인이 있나요?

Is there a discount for first-time customers? - 첫 구매 고객을 위한 할인이 있나요?

I've seen this for less elsewhere. Can you match that price? - 다른 곳에서 이것보다 저렴한 가격에 봤어요. 그 가격에 맞출 수 있나요?

I've seen this for less elsewhere. Can you match that price? - 다른 곳에서 이것보다 저렴한 가격에 봤어요. 그 가격에 맞출 수 있나요?

How much is this with a cash payment? - 현금 결제시 이것의 가격은 얼마인가요?

How much is this with a cash payment? - 현금 결제시 이것의 가격은 얼마인가요?

I'm really interested in this item. Could you give me your best price? - 이 상품에 정말 관심이 있어요. 최선의 가격을 제안해 주실 수 있나요?

I'm really interested in this item. Could you give me your best price? - 이 상품에 정말 관심이 있어요. 최선의 가격을 제안해 주실 수 있나요?

Fashion and Trends:

I love your outfit! Where did you get that jacket? - 당신의 옷차림 정말 멋져요! 그 재킷 어디서 구입하셨나요?

I love your outfit! Where did you get that jacket? - 당신의 옷차림 정말 멋져요! 그 재킷 어디서 구입하셨나요?

This color is really in this season. It would look great on you! - 이 색깔이 이번 시즌에 정말 인기가 많아요. 당신에게 잘 어울릴 거예요!

This color is really in this season. It would look great on you! - 이 색깔이 이번 시즌에 정말 인기가 많아요. 당신에게 잘 어울릴 거예요!

Which of these scarves do you think is more trendy right now? - 이 스카프들 중 어느 것이 지금 더 유행한다고 생각하나요?

Which of these scarves do you think is more trendy right now? - 이 스카프들 중 어느 것이 지금 더 유행한다고 생각하나요?

I'm looking for a gift. What's the most popular item these days? - 선물을 찾고 있어요. 요즘 가장 인기 있는 상품이 무엇인가요?

I'm looking for a gift. What's the most popular item these days? - 선물을 찾고 있어요. 요즘 가장 인기 있는 상품이 무엇인가요?

Do these earrings come in any other colors? - 이 귀걸이 다른 색상으로도 있나요?

Do these earrings come in any other colors? - 이 귀걸이 다른 색상으로도 있나요?

I read that minimalism is coming back. Have you noticed that trend here? - 미니멀리즘이 다시 돌아오고 있다고 들었어요. 여기서도 그 트렌드를 느끼셨나요?

I read that minimalism is coming back. Have you noticed that trend here? - 미니멀리즘이 다시 돌아오고 있다고 들었어요. 여기서도 그 트렌드를 느끼셨나요?

Eating and Drinking:

Can I try the spicy rice cakes, please? - 매운 떡볶이 하나 주세요.

Can I try the spicy rice cakes, please? - 매운 떡볶이 하나 주세요.

What's the most popular snack here? - 여기서 가장 인기 있는 간식이 무엇인가요?

What's the most popular snack here? - 여기서 가장 인기 있는 간식이 무엇인가요?

Can I try the spicy rice cakes, please? - 매운 떡볶이 하나 주세요.

Can I try the spicy rice cakes, please? - 매운 떡볶이 하나 주세요.

What's the most popular snack here? - 여기서 가장 인기 있는 간식이 무엇인가요?

What's the most popular snack here? - 여기서 가장 인기 있는 간식이 무엇인가요?

How much is a serving of kimchi pancakes? - 김치전 한 접시 얼마예요?

How much is a serving of kimchi pancakes? - 김치전 한 접시 얼마예요?

I'd like to try the grilled squid, please. - 구운 오징어 하나 주세요.

I'd like to try the grilled squid, please. - 구운 오징어 하나 주세요.

Does this soup contain seafood? - 이 국에 해산물이 들어가나요?

Does this soup contain seafood? - 이 국에 해산물이 들어가나요?

What ingredients are in this stew? - 이 찌개에 어떤 재료가 들어가나요?

What ingredients are in this stew? - 이 찌개에 어떤 재료가 들어가나요?

Could I have a bottle of water with that, please? - 그것과 함께 물 한 병 주세요.

Could I have a bottle of water with that, please? - 그것과 함께 물 한 병 주세요.

What is the filling in these dumplings? - 이 만두 안에 무엇이 들어가나요?

What is the filling in these dumplings? - 이 만두 안에 무엇이 들어가나요?

Is it possible to make that less spicy? - 그것을 덜 맵게 만들 수 있나요?

Is it possible to make that less spicy? - 그것을 덜 맵게 만들 수 있나요?

I'll have the same as that person, please. - 저 사람이 주문한 것과 똑같은 걸로 주세요.

I'll have the same as that person, please. - 저 사람이 주문한 것과 똑같은 걸로 주세요.

Can I get this to go? - 이것 포장 가능한가요?

Can I get this to go? - 이것 포장 가능한가요?

How long does it take to prepare? - 준비하는데 얼마나 걸리나요?

How long does it take to prepare? - 준비하는데 얼마나 걸리나요?

Do you have any vegetarian options? - 채식 옵션이 있나요?

Do you have any vegetarian options? - 채식 옵션이 있나요?

What's the best way to eat this? - 이것을 먹는 가장 좋은 방법이 무엇인가요?

What's the best way to eat this? - 이것을 먹는 가장 좋은 방법이 무엇인가요?

Can you add extra cheese on top? - 위에 치즈를 추가해 주실 수 있나요?

Can you add extra cheese on top? - 위에 치즈를 추가해 주실 수 있나요?

Is this made fresh daily? - 이것은 매일 신선하게 만드나요?

Is this made fresh daily? - 이것은 매일 신선하게 만드나요?

Navigate Dishes and Ingredients

I'm allergic to peanuts. Does this contain any? - 저는 땅콩에 알레르기가 있어요. 이것에 땅콩이 들어가나요?

I'm allergic to peanuts. Does this contain any? - 저는 땅콩에 알레르기가 있어요. 이것에 땅콩이 들어가나요?

Can you explain what 'bibimbap' is? - '비빔밥'이 무엇인지 설명해 주실 수 있나요?

Can you explain what 'bibimbap' is? - '비빔밥'이 무엇인지 설명해 주실 수 있나요?

Is there a house specialty? - 집에서 특별히 하는 요리가 있나요?

Is there a house specialty? - 집에서 특별히 하는 요리가 있나요?

What's in the seafood pancake? - 해물파전에는 무엇이 들어가나요?

What's in the seafood pancake? - 해물파전에는 무엇이 들어가나요?

Can this dish be made without garlic? - 이 요리를 마늘 없이 만들 수 있나요?

Can this dish be made without garlic? - 이 요리를 마늘 없이 만들 수 있나요?

What kind of meat is used in this dish? - 이 요리에 어떤 종류의 고기가 사용되나요?

What kind of meat is used in this dish? - 이 요리에 어떤 종류의 고기가 사용되나요?

Is the sauce on this spicy? - 이 소스가 맵나요?

Is the sauce on this spicy? - 이 소스가 맵나요?

How is this dish cooked? - 이 요리는 어떻게 조리되나요?

How is this dish cooked? - 이 요리는 어떻게 조리되나요?

Can we get extra side dishes? - 반찬을 추가로 더 얻을 수 있나요?

Can we get extra side dishes? - 반찬을 추가로 더 얻을 수 있나요?

What kind of fish is in this soup? - 이 국에는 어떤 종류의 생선이 들어가나요?

What kind of fish is in this soup? - 이 국에는 어떤 종류의 생선이 들어가나요?

Dining Out

I would like to order the bulgogi, please. - 불고기 주문하고 싶어요. (Bulgogi jumunhago sip-eoyo.)

I would like to order the bulgogi, please. - 불고기 주문하고 싶어요. (Bulgogi jumunhago sip-eoyo.)

Can I have a bowl of bibimbap, please? - 비빔밥 한 그릇 주세요. (Bibimbap han geuleut juseyo.)

Can I have a bowl of bibimbap, please? - 비빔밥 한 그릇 주세요. (Bibimbap han geuleut juseyo.)

I'll have the kimchi jjigae. - 김치찌개 주세요. (Kimchi jjigae juseyo.)

I'll have the kimchi jjigae. - 김치찌개 주세요. (Kimchi jjigae juseyo.)

May I get a serving of japchae, too? - 잡채도 주문할게요. (Japchae-do jumunhalgeyo.)

May I get a serving of japchae, too? - 잡채도 주문할게요. (Japchae-do jumunhalgeyo.)

What are the daily specials? - 오늘의 특별 메뉴가 뭐에요? (Oneul-ui teukbyeol menuga mwoeyo?)

What are the daily specials? - 오늘의 특별 메뉴가 뭐에요? (Oneul-ui teukbyeol menuga mwoeyo?)

I'd like a bottle of water, please. - 물 한 병 주세요. (Mul han byeong juseyo.)

I'd like a bottle of water, please. - 물 한 병 주세요. (Mul han byeong juseyo.)

Do you have any vegetarian options? - 채식주의자용 메뉴 있어요? (Chaesikjuuijayong menyu iss-eoyo?)

Do you have any vegetarian options? - 채식주의자용 메뉴 있어요? (Chaesikjuuijayong menyu iss-eoyo?)

How spicy is the kimchi? - 김치 매운 정도가 어떻게 돼요? (Kimchi maeun jeongdog-a eotteohge dwaeyo?)

How spicy is the kimchi? - 김치 매운 정도가 어떻게 돼요? (Kimchi maeun jeongdog-a eotteohge dwaeyo?)

Can I get some extra soy sauce on the side? - 간장 좀 더 주실 수 있을까요? (Ganjang jom deo jushil su iss-eulkka yo?)

Can I get some extra soy sauce on the side? - 간장 좀 더 주실 수 있을까요? (Ganjang jom deo jushil su iss-eulkka yo?)

For dessert, I'll have the patbingsu. - 디저트로 팥빙수 주세요. (Dijeoteulo patbingsu juseyo.)

For dessert, I'll have the patbingsu. - 디저트로 팥빙수 주세요. (Dijeoteulo patbingsu juseyo.)

I'm allergic to shellfish. - 저는 해산물 알레르기가 있어요. (Jeoneun haesanmul allereugi ga iss-eoyo.)

I'm allergic to shellfish. - 저는 해산물 알레르기가 있어요. (Jeoneun haesanmul allereugi ga iss-eoyo.)

Are there any nuts in this dish? - 이 음식에는 건괴류가 들어가나요? (I eumsig-e-neun gyeongwalyu-ga deul-eogana yo?)

Are there any nuts in this dish? - 이 음식에는 견과류가 들어가나요? (I eumsig-e-neun gyeongwalyu-ga deul-eogana yo?)

I prefer gluten-free options. - 글루텐 프리 옵션을 선호해요. (Geulluteun peuli opseon-eul seonhohae-yo.)

I prefer gluten-free options. - 글루텐 프리 옵션을 선호해요. (Geulluteun peuli opseon-eul seonhohae-yo.)

Does this dish contain dairy? - 이 음식에는 유제품이 들어가나요? (I eumsig-e-neun yujepum-i deul-eogana yo?)

Does this dish contain dairy? - 이 음식에는 유제품이 들어가나요? (I eumsig-e-neun yujepum-i deul-eogana yo?)

I'm a vegetarian, so no meat, please. - 채식주의자라 고기는 제외해 주세요. (Chaesikjuuijala gogineun jeoe-hae juseyo.)

I'm a vegetarian, so no meat, please. - 채식주의자라 고기는 제외해 주세요. (Chaesikjuuijala gogineun jeoe-hae juseyo.)

Is the soup made with chicken broth? - 이 수프는 닭 육수로 만들었나요? (I sup-neun dak yuksu-lo mandeul-eossna yo?)

Is the soup made with chicken broth? - 이 수프는 닭 육수로 만들었나요? (I sup-neun dak yuksu-lo mandeul-eossna yo?)

Could you recommend a dish with no spicy ingredients? - 매운 재료 없는 요리 추천해 주실 수 있나요? (Maewoon jaelo eobsneun yoli chucheonhae jushil su issnayo?)

Could you recommend a dish with no spicy ingredients? - 매운 재료 없는 요리 추천해 주실 수 있나요? (Maewoon jaelo eobsneun yoli chucheonhae jushil su issnayo?)

I avoid caffeine, so is there a decaffeinated option? - 카페인 섭취를 피해요, 디카페인 옵션이 있나요? (Kapein seobchwileul pihaeyo, dikeipein opseoni issnayo?)

I avoid caffeine, so is there a decaffeinated option? - 카페인 섭취를 피해요, 디카페인 옵션이 있나요? (Kapein seobchwileul pihaeyo, dikeipein opseoni issnayo?)

I'm on a low-sodium diet. Can the chef accommodate that? - 저는 저염 식단 중이에요. 요리사가 그에 맞춰줄 수 있을까요? (Jeoneun jeoyeom sikdan jung-ieyo. Yorisaga geu-e matchwojul su iss-eulkka yo?)

I'm on a low-sodium diet. Can the chef accommodate that? - 저는 저염 식단 중이에요. 요리사가 그에 맞춰줄 수 있을까요? (Jeoneun jeoyeom sikdan jung-ieyo. Yorisaga geu-e matchwojul su iss-eulkka yo?)

Is there MSG in any of the dishes? - 음식에 MSG가 들어가 있나요? (Eumsig-e MSG-ga deul-eoga issnayo?)

Is there MSG in any of the dishes? - 음식에 MSG가 들어가 있나요? (Eumsig-e MSG-ga deul-eoga issnayo?)

This dish is delicious! - 이 음식 정말 맛있어요! (I eumsig jeongmal masisseoyo!)

This dish is delicious! - 이 음식 정말 맛있어요! (I eumsig jeongmal masisseoyo!)

The flavors are amazing. - 맛이 너무 훌륭해요. (Masi neomu hullyeonghaeyo.)

The flavors are amazing. - 맛이 너무 훌륭해요. (Masi neomu hullyeonghaeyo.)

The presentation is impressive. - 이 음식의 선물이 인상적이에요. (I eumsig-ui seonmul-i insangjeog-i-e-yo.)

The presentation is impressive. - 이 음식의 선물이 인상적이에요. (I eumsig-ui seonmul-i insangjeog-i-e-yo.)

I'm really enjoying the meal. - 정말 식사를 즐기고 있어요. (Jeongmal sigsareul jeulgigo iss-eoyo.)

I'm really enjoying the meal. - 정말 식사를 즐기고 있어요. (Jeongmal sigsareul jeulgigo iss-eoyo.)

Thank you for the excellent service. - 훌륭한 서비스에 감사합니다. (Hullyeonghan seobiseu-e gamsahamnida.)

Thank you for the excellent service. - 훌륭한 서비스에 감사합니다. (Hullyeonghan seobiseu-e gamsahamnida.)

The food here never disappoints. - 여기 음식은 항상 기대 이상이에요. (Yeogi eumsig-eun hangsang gida isang-i-e-yo.)

The food here never disappoints. - 여기 음식은 항상 기대 이상이에요. (Yeogi eumsig-eun hangsang gida isang-i-e-yo.)

This is one of the best meals I've had. - 이건 내가 먹어본 음식 중에 최고에요. (Igeon naega meog-eobon eumsig jung-e choegoe-yo.)

This is one of the best meals I've had. - 이건 내가 먹어본 음식 중에 최고에요. (Igeon naega meog-eobon eumsig jung-e choegoe-yo.)

The chef has done a fantastic job. - 요리사가 훌륭한 일을 했어요. (Yorisaga hullyeonghan il-eul haess-eoyo.)

The chef has done a fantastic job. - 요리사가 훌륭한 일을 했어요. (Yorisaga hullyeonghan il-eul haess-eoyo.)

I appreciate the attention to detail in every dish. - 모든 음식에서 세심한 주의를 감사히 받아요. (Modeun eumsig-eseo sesimhan juui-reul gamsahi bad-a-yo.)

I appreciate the attention to detail in every dish. - 모든 음식에서 세심한 주의를 감사히 받아요. (Modeun eumsig-eseo sesimhan juui-reul gamsahi bad-a-yo.)

The atmosphere here is perfect for a relaxing meal. - 여기 분위기는 편안한 식사에 딱이에요. (Yeogi bunwigineun pyeonanhan sigsa-e ttak-ieyo.)

The atmosphere here is perfect for a relaxing meal. - 여기 분위기는 편안한 식사에 딱이에요. (Yeogi bunwigineun pyeonanhan sigsa-e ttak-ieyo.)

I'm sorry, but this dish is too salty. - 미안해요, 이 음식이 너무 짜요. (Mianhaeyo, i eumsig-i neomu jayo.)

I'm sorry, but this dish is too salty. - 미안해요, 이 음식이 너무 짜요. (Mianhaeyo, i eumsig-i neomu jayo.)

The meat is a bit overcooked. - 고기가 조금 더 익었어요. (Gogiga jogeum deo igeosseoyo.)

The meat is a bit overcooked. - 고기가 조금 더 익었어요. (Gogiga jogeum deo igeosseoyo.)

I asked for no onions, but they're in the dish. - 양파 빼고 주문했는데, 양파가 들어가 있어요. (Yangpa bbaego jumunhaessneunde, yangpaga deul-eoga iss-eoyo.)

I asked for no onions, but they're in the dish. - 양파 빼고 주문했는데, 양파가 들어가 있어요. (Yangpa bbaego jumunhaessneunde, yangpaga deul-eoga iss-eoyo.)

Can you replace this dish? - 이 음식 대신 다른 걸로 바꿔주실 수 있을까요? (I eumsig daesin dareun geollo bakkwojusil su iss-eulkka yo?)

Can you replace this dish? - 이 음식 대신 다른 걸로 바꿔주실 수 있을까요? (I eumsig daesin dareun geollo bakkwojusil su iss-eulkka yo?)

The service has been slow today. - 오늘 서비스가 느려요. (Oneul seobiseuga neulyeoyo.)

The service has been slow today. - 오늘 서비스가 느려요. (Oneul seobiseuga neulyeoyo.)

I ordered medium rare, but this steak is well-done. - 저는 미디움 레어로 주문했는데, 이 스테이크는 완전히 익었어요. (Jeoneun midium le-eolo jumunhaessneunde, i seuteikeuneun wanjeonhi ig-eosseoyo.)

I ordered medium rare, but this steak is well-done. - 저는 미디움 레어로 주문했는데, 이 스테이크는 완전히 익었어요. (Jeoneun midium le-eolo jumunhaessneunde, i seuteikeuneun wanjeonhi ig-eosseoyo.)

There's a hair in my soup. - 수프에 머리카락이 있어요. (Sup-e meolikarak-i iss-eoyo.)

There's a hair in my soup. - 수프에 머리카락이 있어요. (Sup-e meolikarak-i iss-eoyo.)

The portion size is too small for the price. - 양이 비싼 가격에 비해 작아요. (Yang-i bissan gageum-e bihae jag-ayo.)

The portion size is too small for the price. - 양이 비싼 가격에 비해 작아요. (Yang-i bissan gageum-e bihae jag-ayo.)

The dessert was disappointing. - 디저트가 실망스러웠어요. (Dijeoteu-ga silmangseuleowosseoyo.)

The dessert was disappointing. - 디저트가 실망스러웠어요. (Dijeoteu-ga silmangseuleowosseoyo.)

I think there might be a mistake in my order. - 주문에 실수가 있을 것 같아요. (Jumun-e silsu-ga iss-eul geos gatayo.)

I think there might be a mistake in my order. - 주문에 실수가 있을 것 같아요. (Jumun-e silsu-ga iss-eul geos gatayo.)

What's the chef's specialty? - 요리사 특별 메뉴가 뭐에요? (Yorisaga teukbyeol menuga mwoeyo?)

What's the chef's specialty? - 요리사 특별 메뉴가 뭐에요? (Yorisaga teukbyeol menuga mwoeyo?)

I'll go for the spicy seafood stew, please. - 매운 해물 찌개로 주문할게요. (Maewoon haemul jjigae-lo jumunhalgeyo.)

I'll go for the spicy seafood stew, please. - 매운 해물 찌개로 주문할게요. (Maewoon haemul jjigae-lo jumunhalgeyo.)

Can I have a side of kimchi with my meal? - 식사에 김치 좀 추가해 주세요. (Sigsae gimchi jom chugae juseyo.)

Can I have a side of kimchi with my meal? - 식사에 김치 좀 추가해 주세요. (Sigsae gimchi jom chugae juseyo.)

Is it possible to make that dish less spicy? - 그 음식을 좀 덜 매워 만들 수 있을까요? (Geu eumsig-eul jom deol maewo mandeul su iss-eulkka yo?)

Is it possible to make that dish less spicy? - 그 음식을 좀 덜 매워 만들 수 있을까요? (Geu eumsig-eul jom deol maewo mandeul su iss-eulkka yo?)

I'll try the bulgogi set menu. - 불고기 세트 메뉴 시도해 볼게요. (Bulgogi seteu menyu sidohae bolgeyo.)

I'll try the bulgogi set menu. - 불고기 세트 메뉴 시도해 볼게요. (Bulgogi seteu menyu sidohae bolgeyo.)

I'm in the mood for something sweet. What do you recommend for dessert? - 달콤한 걸 먹고 싶어요. 디저트로 뭐 추천해 주세요? (Dalkomhan geol meokgo sip-eoyo. Dijeoteulo mwo chucheonhae juseyo?)

I'm in the mood for something sweet. What do you recommend for dessert? - 달콤한 걸 먹고 싶어요. 디저트로 뭐 추천해 주세요? (Dalkomhan geol meokgo sip-eoyo. Dijeoteulo mwo chucheonhae juseyo?)

Could you make my dish without any garlic, please? - 제 음식에는 마늘 하나도 넣지 말아 주시겠어요? (Je eumsig-eneun maneul hanado neohji mala jushigess-eoyo?)

Could you make my dish without any garlic, please? - 제 음식에는 마늘 하나도 넣지 말아 주시겠어요? (Je eumsig-eneun maneul hanado neohji mala jushigess-eoyo?)

What's the house specialty drink? - 집에서 만든 특별 음료가 뭐에요? (Jib-eseo mandeun teukbyeol eumnyo-ga mwoeyo?)

What's the house specialty drink? - 집에서 만든 특별 음료가 뭐에요? (Jib-eseo mandeun teukbyeol eumnyo-ga mwoeyo?)

Is tap water safe to drink here? - 이곳의 수돗물 마셔도 괜찮아요? (Igos-ui sudotmul mas-eodo gwaenchanh-a-yo?)

Is tap water safe to drink here? - 이곳의 수돗물 마셔도 괜찮아요? (Igos-ui sudotmul mas-eodo gwaenchanh-a-yo?)

I'd like to order a green tea, please. - 녹차 한 잔 주세요. (Nokcha han jan juseyo.)

I'd like to order a green tea, please. - 녹차 한 잔 주세요. (Nokcha han jan juseyo.)

I have a lactose intolerance, so no dairy, please. - 제가 유당 알레르기가 있어서 유제품은 빼 주세요. (Jega yudang allereugi-ga iss-eoseo yuje-pum-eun ppae juseyo.)

I have a lactose intolerance, so no dairy, please. - 제가 유당 알레르기가 있어서 유제품은 빼 주세요. (Jega yudang allereugi-ga iss-eoseo yuje-pum-eun ppae juseyo.)

Is there an option for gluten-free bread? - 글루텐
프리 빵으로 바꿔도 될까요? (Geulluteun peuli
ppang-eulo bakkwodo doelkkayo?)

Is there an option for gluten-free bread? - 글루텐
프리 빵으로 바꿔도 될까요? (Geulluteun peuli
ppang-eulo bakkwodo doelkkayo?)

Can I get the salad dressing on the side? - 샐러드
드레싱은 따로 주실 수 있을까요? (Saelladeu
deuresingeun ttalo jushil su iss-eulkka yo?)

Can I get the salad dressing on the side? - 샐러드
드레싱은 따로 주실 수 있을까요? (Saelladeu
deuresingeun ttalo jushil su iss-eulkka yo?)

I'm on a low-carb diet, so please no rice or pasta. -
제가 저탄수화물 식단이라 밥이나 파스타는
제외해 주세요. (Jega jeo tansuhwamul sikdan-il-a
bab-ina paseuta-neun jeoe-hae juseyo.)

I'm on a low-carb diet, so please no rice or pasta. -
제가 저탄수화물 식단이라 밥이나 파스타는
제외해 주세요. (Jega jeo tansuhwamul sikdan-il-a
bab-ina paseuta-neun jeoe-hae juseyo.)

Is the curry vegetarian-friendly? - 카레에는
채식주의자용 메뉴가 있나요? (Kale-e-neun
chaesikjuuijayong menyu ga issnayo?)

Is the curry vegetarian-friendly? - 카레에는
채식주의자용 메뉴가 있나요? (Kale-e-neun
chaesikjuuijayong menyu ga issnayo?)

Are there any dishes suitable for someone with a peanut allergy? - 땅콩 알레르기가 있는 사람을 위한 음식이 있나요? (Ttangkong allereugi-ga issneun salam-eul wihan eumsig-i issnayo?)

Are there any dishes suitable for someone with a peanut allergy? - 땅콩 알레르기가 있는 사람을 위한 음식이 있나요? (Ttangkong allereugi-ga issneun salam-eul wihan eumsig-i issnayo?)

I prefer my steak medium-rare. - 제 스테이크는 미디움 레어로 주문할게요. (Je seuteikeu-neun midium le-eolo jumunhalgeyo.)

I prefer my steak medium-rare. - 제 스테이크는 미디움 레어로 주문할게요. (Je seuteikeu-neun midium le-eolo jumunhalgeyo.)

Is it possible to have the sauce on the side? - 소스는 따로 주문할 수 있을까요? (Soseu-neun ttalo jumunhal su iss-eulkka yo?)

Is it possible to have the sauce on the side? - 소스는 따로 주문할 수 있을까요? (Soseu-neun ttalo jumunhal su iss-eulkka yo?)

I'm trying to cut down on sugar, so can you make my drink less sweet? - 설탕 섭취를 줄이려고 하는데, 음료를 덜 달게 만들 수 있을까요? (Setang seobchwileul jul-ilyeogo haneunde, eumlyo-leul deol dalge mandeul su iss-eulkka yo?)

I'm trying to cut down on sugar, so can you make my drink less sweet? - 설탕 섭취를 줄이려고 하는데, 음료를 덜 달게 만들 수 있을까요? (Setang seobchwileul jul-ilyeogo haneunde, eumlyo-leul deol dalge mandeul su iss-eulkka yo?)

Is there a vegan option on the menu? - 메뉴 중에 비건 옵션이 있나요? (Menyu jung-e bigeon opseoi issnayo?)

Is there a vegan option on the menu? - 메뉴 중에 비건 옵션이 있나요? (Menyu jung-e bigeon opseoi issnayo?)

The presentation of this dish is exquisite! - 이 음식의 프레젠테이션이 정말 훌륭해요! (I eumsig-ui peulejenteisyeoni jeongmal hullyeonghaeyo!)

The presentation of this dish is exquisite! - 이 음식의 프레젠테이션이 정말 훌륭해요! (I eumsig-ui peulejenteisyeoni jeongmal hullyeonghaeyo!)

I can taste the freshness of the ingredients. - 식재료의 신선함을 느낄 수 있어요. (Sigjaelyo-ui sinsanham-eul neukkil su iss-eoyo.)

I can taste the freshness of the ingredients. - 식재료의 신선함을 느낄 수 있어요. (Sigjaelyo-ui sinsanham-eul neukkil su iss-eoyo.)

The balance of flavors is perfect. - 맛의 균형이 완벽해요. (Mat-ui gyunhyeong-i wanbyeoghaeyo.)

The balance of flavors is perfect. - 맛의 균형이 완벽해요. (Mat-ui gyunhyeong-i wanbyeoghaeyo.)

The portion size is just right. - 양이 딱 적당해요. (Yang-i ttak jeogdanghaeyo.)

The portion size is just right. - 양이 딱 적당해요. (Yang-i ttak jeogdanghaeyo.)

I appreciate the chef's attention to detail. - 요리사의 세심한 손길이 감사돼요. (Yorisayi sesimhan songili gamsadwaeyo.)

I appreciate the chef's attention to detail. - 요리사의 세심한 손길이 감사돼요. (Yorisayi sesimhan songili gamsadwaeyo.)

The atmosphere in this restaurant is very inviting. - 이 식당의 분위기가 정말 매력적이에요. (I sigdang-ui bunwigiga jeongmal maeryeogjeog-ieyo.)

The atmosphere in this restaurant is very inviting. - 이 식당의 분위기가 정말 매력적이에요. (I sigdang-ui bunwigiga jeongmal maeryeogjeog-ieyo.)

I'm delighted with the diverse menu options. - 다양한 메뉴 옵션에 만족해요. (Dayanghan menyu opseon-e manjokhaeyo.)

I'm delighted with the diverse menu options. - 다양한 메뉴 옵션에 만족해요. (Dayanghan menyu opseon-e manjokhaeyo.)

The service has been exceptional tonight. - 오늘 서비스가 특별히 좋았어요. (Oneul seobiseuga teukbyeolhi joh-ass-eoyo.)

The service has been exceptional tonight. - 오늘 서비스가 특별히 좋았어요. (Oneul seobiseuga teukbyeolhi joh-ass-eoyo.)

The dessert is the perfect way to end the meal. - 디저트는 식사를 완벽하게 마무리하는 방법이에요. (Dijeoteuneun sigsal-eul wanbyeogage mamuli-haneun bangbeob-ieyo.)

The dessert is the perfect way to end the meal. - 디저트는 식사를 완벽하게 마무리하는 방법이에요. (Dijeoteuneun sigsal-eul wanbyeogage mamuli-haneun bangbeob-ieyo.)

I'll definitely recommend this place to my friends. - 내 친구들에게 이곳을 꼭 추천할게요. (Nae chingudeul-ege igos-eul kkok chucheonhalgeyo.)

I'll definitely recommend this place to my friends. - 내 친구들에게 이곳을 꼭 추천할게요. (Nae chingudeul-ege igos-eul kkok chucheonhalgeyo.)

I ordered this dish without salt, but it's still salty. - 이 음식에는 소금 없이 주문했는데, 여전히 짜요. (I eumsig-eneun sog-eum eobs-i jumunhaessneunde, yeojeonhi jayo.)

I ordered this dish without salt, but it's still salty. - 이 음식에는 소금 없이 주문했는데, 여전히 짜요. (I eumsig-eneun sog-eum eobs-i jumunhaessneunde, yeojeonhi jayo.)

The dish was too bland for my taste. - 제 입맛에는 이 음식이 너무 싱겁게 느껴져요. (Je ibmas-e-neun i eumsig-i neomu sing-geopge neukkyeojyeoyo.)

The dish was too bland for my taste. - 제 입맛에는 이 음식이 너무 싱겁게 느껴져요. (Je ibmas-e-neun i eumsig-i neomu sing-geopge neukkyeojyeoyo.)

I expected more seasoning in this dish. - 이 음식에는 더 많은 향신료가 들어갈 줄 알았어요. (I eumsig-eneun deo manh-eun hyangsinlyo-ga deul-eogal jul al-ass-eoyo.)

I expected more seasoning in this dish. - 이 음식에는 더 많은 향신료가 들어갈 줄 알았어요. (I eumsig-eneun deo manh-eun hyangsinlyo-ga deul-eogal jul al-ass-eoyo.)

The dessert didn't meet my expectations. - 디저트는 제 기대에 미치지 못했어요. (Dijeoteuneun je gidae-e michi mothaess-eoyo.)

The dessert didn't meet my expectations. - 디저트는 제 기대에 미치지 못했어요. (Dijeoteuneun je gidae-e michi mothaess-eoyo.)

The wait for our table was longer than anticipated. - 테이블 기다리는 시간이 예상보다 더 길었어요. (Teibeul gidarineun sigan-i yesangboda deo gil-eoss-eoyo.)

The wait for our table was longer than anticipated. - 테이블 기다리는 시간이 예상보다 더 길었어요. (Teibeul gidarineun sigan-i yesangboda deo gil-eoss-eoyo.)

I found a small bone in my fish. - 생선에 작은 뼈가 있었어요. (Saengson-e jageun ppyeoga iss-eoss-eoyo.)

I found a small bone in my fish. - 생선에 작은 뼈가 있었어요. (Saengson-e jageun ppyeoga iss-eoss-eoyo.)

The temperature of the food was not consistent. - 음식의 온도가 일정하지 않았어요. (Eumsig-ui ondo-ga iljeonghaji anh-ass-eoyo.)

The temperature of the food was not consistent. - 음식의 온도가 일정하지 않았어요. (Eumsig-ui ondo-ga iljeonghaji anh-ass-eoyo.)

The service tonight has been disappointing. - 오늘 서비스가 기대에 못 미쳤어요. (Oneul seobiseuga gidae-e mot michyeoss-eoyo.)

The service tonight has been disappointing. - 오늘 서비스가 기대에 못 미쳤어요. (Oneul seobiseuga gidae-e mot michyeoss-eoyo.)

I asked for no cilantro, but it's in the dish. - 코리앤더 빼고 주문했는데, 안에 들어가 있어요. (Koliandeo bbaego jumunhaessneunde, an-e deul-eoga iss-eoyo.)

I asked for no cilantro, but it's in the dish. - 코리앤더 빼고 주문했는데, 안에 들어가 있어요. (Koliandeo bbaego jumunhaessneunde, an-e deul-eoga iss-eoyo.)

I'm afraid I cannot recommend this place based on my experience. - 제 경험을 바탕으로 이곳을 추천하기 힘들어요. (Je gyeongheom-eul batang-eulo igos-eul chucheonhagi himdeuleoyo.)

I'm afraid I cannot recommend this place based on my experience. - 제 경험을 바탕으로 이곳을 추천하기 힘들어요. (Je gyeongheom-eul batang-eulo igos-eul chucheonhagi himdeuleoyo.)

Making Friends and Socializing

Hi, how are you? - 안녕, 어떻게 지내? (Annyeong, eotteoke jinae?)

Hi, how are you? - 안녕, 어떻게 지내? (Annyeong, eotteoke jinae?)

My name is [Name]. - 제 이름은 [이름]입니다. (Je ireumeun [ireum]imnida.)

My name is [Name]. - 제 이름은 [이름]입니다. (Je ireumeun [ireum]imnida.)

What's your name? - 당신의 이름은 무엇인가요? (Dangsinui ireumeun mueosingayo?)

What's your name? - 당신의 이름은 무엇인가요? (Dangsinui ireumeun mueosingayo?)

Nice to meet you. - 만나서 반가워요. (Mannaseo bangawoyo.)

Nice to meet you. - 만나서 반가워요. (Mannaseo bangawoyo.)

Do you come here often? - 여기 자주 오시나요? (Yeogi jaju osinayo?)

Do you come here often? - 여기 자주 오시나요? (Yeogi jaju osinayo?)

I'm from [Country]. - 저는 [국가]에서 왔어요. (Jeoneun [gukga]eseo wasseoyo.)

I'm from [Country]. - 저는 [국가]에서 왔어요. (Jeoneun [gukga]eseo wasseoyo.)

What do you do for fun? - 무엇을 하면서 재미를 느껴요? (Mueoseul hamyeonseo jaemireul neukkyeoyo?)

What do you do for fun? - 무엇을 하면서 재미를 느껴요? (Mueoseul hamyeonseo jaemireul neukkyeoyo?)

Would you like to join us? - 우리와 함께 하시겠어요? (Uriwa hamkke hasigesseoyo?)

Would you like to join us? - 우리와 함께 하시겠어요? (Uriwa hamkke hasigesseoyo?)

I love your [item]. - 당신의 [아이템]이 정말 좋네요. (Dangsinui [aitem]i jeongmal johneyo.)

I love your [item]. - 당신의 [아이템]이 정말 좋네요. (Dangsinui [aitem]i jeongmal johneyo.)

Can I buy you a drink? - 당신에게 음료를 사도 될까요? (Dangsinege eumryoreul sado doelkkayo?)

Can I buy you a drink? - 당신에게 음료를 사도 될까요? (Dangsinege eumryoreul sado doelkkayo?)

Do you have any hobbies? - 취미가 무엇인가요? (Chwimiga mueosingayo?)

Do you have any hobbies? - 취미가 무엇인가요? (Chwimiga mueosingayo?)

What kind of music do you like? - 어떤 종류의 음악을 좋아하나요? (Eotteon jongryueui eumageul joahanayo?)

What kind of music do you like? - 어떤 종류의 음악을 좋아하나요? (Eotteon jongryueui eumageul joahanayo?)

Have you seen any good movies lately? - 최근에 좋은 영화 본 게 있나요? (Choegune joheun yeonghwa bon ge issnayo?)

Have you seen any good movies lately? - 최근에 좋은 영화 본 게 있나요? (Choegune joheun yeonghwa bon ge issnayo?)

I'm trying to improve my Korean. - 저는 한국어 실력을 향상시키려고 해요. (Jeoneun hangugeo sillyeogeul hyangsangshikiryeogo haeyo.)

I'm trying to improve my Korean. - 저는 한국어 실력을 향상시키려고 해요. (Jeoneun hangugeo sillyeogeul hyangsangshikiryeogo haeyo.)

Can you recommend a good restaurant here? - 여기 좋은 식당 추천해 줄 수 있나요? (Yeogi joheun sikdang chucheonhae jul su issnayo?)

Can you recommend a good restaurant here? - 여기 좋은 식당 추천해 줄 수 있나요? (Yeogi joheun sikdang chucheonhae jul su issnayo?)

I'm looking for a language exchange partner. - 저는 언어 교환 파트너를 찾고 있어요. (Jeoneun eoneo gyohwan partneoreul chatgo isseoyo.)

I'm looking for a language exchange partner. - 저는 언어 교환 파트너를 찾고 있어요. (Jeoneun eoneo gyohwan partneoreul chatgo isseoyo.)

Would you like to grab coffee sometime? - 언젠가 커피 한 잔 할래요? (Eonjenga keopi han jan hallaeyo?)

Would you like to grab coffee sometime? - 언젠가 커피 한 잔 할래요? (Eonjenga keopi han jan hallaeyo?)

What brings you here today? - 오늘 여기에 온 이유가 무엇인가요? (Oneul yeogie on iyuga mueosingayo?)

What brings you here today? - 오늘 여기에 온 이유가 무엇인가요? (Oneul yeogie on iyuga mueosingayo?)

Do you want to go out for dinner together? - 같이 저녁 식사하러 갈래요? (Gati jeonyeok sikshareo gallaeyo?)

Do you want to go out for dinner together? - 같이 저녁 식사하러 갈래요? (Gati jeonyeok sikshareo gallaeyo?)

Let's exchange contact information. - 연락처를 교환합시다. (Yeonrakcheoreul gyohwahabsida.)

Let's exchange contact information. - 연락처를 교환합시다. (Yeonrakcheoreul gyohwahabsida.)

It's been great talking with you. - 당신과 대화하는 것이 정말 좋았어요. (Dangsingwa daehwahaneun geosi jeongmal johasseoyo.)

It's been great talking with you. - 당신과 대화하는 것이 정말 좋았어요. (Dangsingwa daehwahaneun geosi jeongmal johasseoyo.)

We should hang out again soon. - 우리 곧 다시 만나서 놀아야 해요. (Uri got dasi mannaseo noraya haeyo.)

We should hang out again soon. - 우리 곧 다시 만나서 놀아야 해요. (Uri got dasi mannaseo noraya haeyo.)

Can you teach me some Korean? - 저에게 한국어를 좀 가르쳐 줄 수 있나요? (Jeoege hangugeoreul jom gareuchyeo jul su issnayo?)

Can you teach me some Korean? - 저에게 한국어를 좀 가르쳐 줄 수 있나요? (Jeoege hangugeoreul jom gareuchyeo jul su issnayo?)

I'm glad we met. - 우리가 만난 게 기쁘네요. (Uriga mannange gippeuneyo.)

I'm glad we met. - 우리가 만난 게 기쁘네요. (Uriga mannange gippeuneyo.)

Let's take a photo together. - 함께 사진 찍읍시다. (Hamkke sajin jjigeupsida.)

Let's take a photo together. - 함께 사진 찍읍시다. (Hamkke sajin jjigeupsida.)

Medical Emergencies and Health Care

I need a doctor. - 의사가 필요해요.

I need a doctor. - 의사가 필요해요.

Is there a hospital nearby? - 근처에 병원이 있나요?

Is there a hospital nearby? - 근처에 병원이 있나요?

I have an allergy. - 알레르기가 있어요.
I have an allergy. - 알레르기가 있어요.

Please call an ambulance. - 구급차를 불러주세요.
Please call an ambulance. - 구급차를 불러주세요.

I am in pain. - 아픕니다.
I am in pain. - 아픕니다.

I have a fever. - 열이 있어요.
I have a fever. - 열이 있어요.

I feel dizzy. - 어지러워요.
I feel dizzy. - 어지러워요.

I need medicine. - 약이 필요해요.
I need medicine. - 약이 필요해요

Where is the pharmacy? - 약국이 어디예요?

Where is the pharmacy? - 약국이 어디예요?

I have a headache. - 머리가 아파요.
I have a headache. - 머리가 아파요.

Can you help me? - 도와줄 수 있나요?
Can you help me? - 도와줄 수 있나요?

I need to see a specialist. - 전문의를 만나야 해요.

I need to see a specialist. - 전문의를 만나야 해요.

It's an emergency. - 긴급한 상황이에요.
It's an emergency. - 긴급한 상황이에요.

I'm allergic to penicillin. - 페니실린에 알레르기가 있어요.
I'm allergic to penicillin. - 페니실린에 알레르기가 있어요.

Do you accept insurance? - 보험 적용이 되나요?
Do you accept insurance? - 보험 적용이 되나요?

I need an appointment. - 예약이 필요해요.
I need an appointment. - 예약이 필요해요.

Where is the emergency room? - 응급실이 어디에 있나요?
Where is the emergency room? - 응급실이 어디에 있나요?

I have chest pain. - 가슴이 아파요.
I have chest pain. - 가슴이 아파요.

I am having trouble breathing. - 숨쉬기가 어려워요.

I am having trouble breathing. - 숨쉬기가 어려워요.

Is it serious? - 심각한가요?
Is it serious? - 심각한가요?

I have a toothache. - 이가 아파요.
I have a toothache. - 이가 아파요.

Can I get a prescription? - 처방전을 받을 수 있나요?
Can I get a prescription? - 처방전을 받을 수 있나요?

I need a refill. - 약을 추가로 필요해요.
I need a refill. - 약을 추가로 필요해요.

Where can I get tested? - 어디에서 검사를 받을 수 있나요?

Where can I get tested? - 어디에서 검사를 받을 수 있나요?

I think it's broken. - 부러진 것 같아요.
I think it's broken. - 부러진 것 같아요.

Do I need surgery? - 수술이 필요한가요?
Do I need surgery? - 수술이 필요한가요?

How long will the recovery take? - 회복하는 데 얼마나 걸리나요?

How long will the recovery take? - 회복하는 데 얼마나 걸리나요?

I need to cancel my appointment. - 예약을 취소해야 해요.
I need to cancel my appointment. - 예약을 취소해야 해요.

Can I speak to a doctor? - 의사와 대화할 수 있나요?

Can I speak to a doctor? - 의사와 대화할 수 있나요?

I'm here for my appointment. - 제 예약 때문에 왔어요.

I'm here for my appointment. - 제 예약 때문에 왔어요.

Handling Money and Banking

How much does this cost? - 이거 얼마예요? (Igeo eolmayeyo?)

How much does this cost? - 이거 얼마예요? (Igeo eolmayeyo?)

Can I have the bill, please? - 계산서 부탁드려요. (Gyesanseo butakdeuryeoyo.)

Can I have the bill, please? - 계산서 부탁드려요. (Gyesanseo butakdeuryeoyo.)

Where is the nearest ATM? - 가장 가까운 ATM 어디에 있나요? (Gajang gakkaun ATM eodie issnayo?)

Where is the nearest ATM? - 가장 가까운 ATM 어디에 있나요? (Gajang gakkaun ATM eodie issnayo?)

I would like to open a bank account. - 은행 계좌를 개설하고 싶어요. (Eunhaeng gyejwareul gaeseolhago sipeoyo.)

I would like to open a bank account. - 은행 계좌를 개설하고 싶어요. (Eunhaeng gyejwareul gaeseolhago sipeoyo.)

Can I exchange money here? - 여기서 환전할 수 있나요? (Yeogiseo hwanjeonhal su issnayo?)
 Can I exchange money here? - 여기서 환전할 수 있나요? (Yeogiseo hwanjeonhal su issnayo?)

What is the exchange rate? - 환율이 얼마인가요? (Hwanyuri eolmaingayo?)
 What is the exchange rate? - 환율이 얼마인가요? (Hwanyuri eolmaingayo?)

I need to transfer money. - 돈을 송금해야 해요. (Doneul songgeumhaeya haeyo.)
 I need to transfer money. - 돈을 송금해야 해요. (Doneul songgeumhaeya haeyo.)

Can I get this in smaller bills? - 이걸 작은 지폐로 바꿀 수 있나요? (Igeol jageun jipyeoro bakkul su issnayo?)
 Can I get this in smaller bills? - 이걸 작은 지폐로 바꿀 수 있나요? (Igeol jageun jipyeoro bakkul su issnayo?)

Is there a fee for this service? - 이 서비스에 수수료가 붙나요? (I seobiseue susuryoga butnayo?)
 Is there a fee for this service? - 이 서비스에 수수료가 붙나요? (I seobiseue susuryoga butnayo?)

I lost my credit card. - 신용카드를 잃어버렸어요. (Sinyongkadeureul ilheobeoryeosseoyo.)
I lost my credit card. - 신용카드를 잃어버렸어요. (Sinyongkadeureul ilheobeoryeosseoyo.)

I need to withdraw some money. - 돈을 좀 인출해야 해요. (Doneul jom inchulhaeya haeyo.)
I need to withdraw some money. - 돈을 좀 인출해야 해요. (Doneul jom inchulhaeya haeyo.)

What is my account balance? - 제 계좌 잔액이 얼마인가요? (Je gyejwa janagi eolmaingayo?)
What is my account balance? - 제 계좌 잔액이 얼마인가요? (Je gyejwa janagi eolmaingayo?)

Can I have a receipt, please? - 영수증 주실 수 있나요? (Yeongsujeung jusil su issnayo?)
Can I have a receipt, please? - 영수증 주실 수 있나요? (Yeongsujeung jusil su issnayo?)

I would like to deposit this check. - 이 수표를 입금하고 싶어요. (I supyoreul ipgeumhago sipeoyo.)
I would like to deposit this check. - 이 수표를 입금하고 싶어요. (I supyoreul ipgeumhago sipeoyo.)

How do I apply for a loan? - 대출은 어떻게 신청하나요? (Daechuleun eotteoke sincheonghanayo?)
How do I apply for a loan? - 대출은 어떻게 신청하나요? (Daechuleun eotteoke sincheonghanayo?)

I need to change my PIN. - 제 PIN 번호를 변경해야 해요. (Je PIN beonhoreul byeongyeonghaeya haeyo.)
 I need to change my PIN. - 제 PIN 번호를 변경해야 해요. (Je PIN beonhoreul byeongyeonghaeya haeyo.)

Can you lock my account? - 제 계좌를 잠글 수 있나요? (Je gyejwareul jamgeul su issnayo?)
 Can you lock my account? - 제 계좌를 잠글 수 있나요? (Je gyejwareul jamgeul su issnayo?)

I'd like to check my transaction history. - 거래 내역을 확인하고 싶어요. (Georae naeyageul hwakinhago sipeoyo.)
 I'd like to check my transaction history. - 거래 내역을 확인하고 싶어요. (Georae naeyageul hwakinhago sipeoyo.)

What's the limit on this card? - 이 카드의 한도가 얼마인가요? (I kadeuui handoga eolmaingayo?)
 What's the limit on this card? - 이 카드의 한도가 얼마인가요? (I kadeuui handoga eolmaingayo?)

Could you help me with online banking? - 온라인 뱅킹을 도와주실 수 있나요? (Onlain baengkingeul dowajusil su issnayo?)
 Could you help me with online banking? - 온라인 뱅킹을 도와주실 수 있나요? (Onlain baengkingeul dowajusil su issnayo?)

I need a statement for the last three months. - 지난 세 달 동안의 계좌 명세서가 필요해요. (Jinan se

dal donganui gyejwa myeongsesoga piryohaeyo.)
 I need a statement for the last three months. - 지난
세 달 동안의 계좌 명세서가 필요해요. (Jinan se
dal donganui gyejwa myeongsesoga piryohaeyo.)

Is this card accepted internationally? - 이 카드는
국제적으로 사용할 수 있나요? (I kadeuneun
gukjejeogeuro sayonghal su issnayo?)
 Is this card accepted internationally? - 이 카드는
국제적으로 사용할 수 있나요? (I kadeuneun
gukjejeogeuro sayonghal su issnayo?)

I'd like to report a lost checkbook. - 분실된
수표장을 신고하고 싶어요. (Bunsildoen
supyojangeul singohago sipeoyo.)
 I'd like to report a lost checkbook. - 분실된
수표장을 신고하고 싶어요. (Bunsildoen
supyojangeul singohago sipeoyo.)

How do I use this banking app? - 이 뱅킹 앱을
어떻게 사용하나요? (I baengking aeb-eul eotteoke
sayonghanayo?)
 How do I use this banking app? - 이 뱅킹 앱을
어떻게 사용하나요? (I baengking aeb-eul eotteoke
sayonghanayo?)

Can I have a loan extension? - 대출 기간 연장이
가능한가요? (Daechul gigan yeonjangi
ganeunghangayo?)
 Can I have a loan extension? - 대출 기간 연장이
가능한가요? (Daechul gigan yeonjangi
ganeunghangayo?)

What are the charges for international transfers? - 국제 송금 수수료는 얼마인가요? (Gukje songgeum susuryoneun eolmaingayo?)

 What are the charges for international transfers? - 국제 송금 수수료는 얼마인가요? (Gukje songgeum susuryoneun eolmaingayo?)

I'd like to close my account. - 제 계좌를 폐쇄하고 싶어요. (Je gyejwareul pyeswaehago sipeoyo.)

 I'd like to close my account. - 제 계좌를 폐쇄하고 싶어요. (Je gyejwareul pyeswaehago sipeoyo.)

Can I set up a direct debit? - 직불 설정이 가능한가요? (Jikbul seoljeongi ganeunghangayo?)

 Can I set up a direct debit? - 직불 설정이 가능한가요? (Jikbul seoljeongi ganeunghangayo?)

How can I protect my account from fraud? - 제 계좌를 사기로부터 어떻게 보호할 수 있나요? (Je gyejwareul sagirobuteo eotteoke bohohal su issnayo?)

 How can I protect my account from fraud? - 제 계좌를 사기로부터 어떻게 보호할 수 있나요? (Je gyejwareul sagirobuteo eotteoke bohohal su issnayo?)

Job Hunting and Workplace Language

Can I have your business card? 명함을 주실 수 있나요?

Can I have your business card? 명함을 주실 수 있나요?

I am interested in this position. 이 직위에 관심이 있습니다.

I am interested in this position. 이 직위에 관심이 있습니다.

What are the job requirements? 직무 요건은 무엇인가요?

What are the job requirements? 직무 요건은 무엇인가요?

When is the application deadline? 지원 마감 기한은 언제인가요?

When is the application deadline? 지원 마감 기한은 언제인가요?

Could you tell me more about the team I'll be working with? 제가 일하게 될 팀에 대해 더 말씀해 주실 수 있나요?

Could you tell me more about the team I'll be working with? 제가 일하게 될 팀에 대해 더 말씀해 주실 수 있나요?

How would you describe the company culture? 회사 문화를 어떻게 설명하시겠어요?

How would you describe the company culture? 회사 문화를 어떻게 설명하시겠어요?

What are the next steps in the hiring process? 채용 과정의 다음 단계는 무엇인가요?

What are the next steps in the hiring process?
채용 과정의 다음 단계는 무엇인가요?

I look forward to hearing from you. 답변
기다리겠습니다.

I look forward to hearing from you. 답변
기다리겠습니다.

Thank you for the opportunity to interview. 면접
기회를 주셔서 감사합니다.

Thank you for the opportunity to interview. 면접
기회를 주셔서 감사합니다.

I am very enthusiastic about joining your team.
귀사의 팀에 합류하는 것에 대해 매우
열정적입니다.

I am very enthusiastic about joining your team.
귀사의 팀에 합류하는 것에 대해 매우
열정적입니다.

Can we discuss the salary range? 급여 범위에
대해 논의할 수 있나요?

Can we discuss the salary range? 급여 범위에
대해 논의할 수 있나요?

Are there opportunities for advancement? 승진
기회가 있나요?

Are there opportunities for advancement? 승진
기회가 있나요?

Is there a work-from-home option? 재택근무 옵션이 있나요?

Is there a work-from-home option? 재택근무 옵션이 있나요?

What is the feedback process like here? 여기서의 피드백 과정은 어떤가요?

What is the feedback process like here? 여기서의 피드백 과정은 어떤가요?

Can you tell me about work-life balance at the company? 회사에서의 워크-라이프 밸런스에 대해 말씀해 주실 수 있나요?

Can you tell me about work-life balance at the company? 회사에서의 워크-라이프 밸런스에 대해 말씀해 주실 수 있나요?

What training programs do you offer? 어떤 교육 프로그램을 제공하나요?

What training programs do you offer? 어떤 교육 프로그램을 제공하나요?

Who will I report to? 누구에게 보고해야 하나요?

Who will I report to? 누구에게 보고해야 하나요?

Can you describe a typical day in this role? 이 역할에서의 전형적인 하루를 설명해 주실 수 있나요?

Can you describe a typical day in this role? 이 역할에서의 전형적인 하루를 설명해 주실 수 있나요?

What are the biggest challenges the team faces? 팀이 직면한 가장 큰 도전은 무엇인가요?

What are the biggest challenges the team faces? 팀이 직면한 가장 큰 도전은 무엇인가요?

How do you measure success in this position? 이 직위에서 성공을 어떻게 측정하나요?

How do you measure success in this position? 이 직위에서 성공을 어떻게 측정하나요?

Are there regular team meetings? 정기적인 팀 회의가 있나요?

Are there regular team meetings? 정기적인 팀 회의가 있나요?

What is the company's policy on remote work? 회사의 원격 근무 정책은 무엇인가요?

What is the company's policy on remote work? 회사의 원격 근무 정책은 무엇인가요?

How does the company support employee growth? 회사는 직원 성장을 어떻게 지원하나요?

How does the company support employee growth? 회사는 직원 성장을 어떻게 지원하나요?

Is there a mentorship program? 멘토링 프로그램이 있나요?

Is there a mentorship program? 멘토링 프로그램이 있나요?

What kind of performance reviews do you have? 어떤 종류의 성과 평가가 있나요?

What kind of performance reviews do you have? 어떤 종류의 성과 평가가 있나요?

How does the company recognize outstanding achievements? 회사는 뛰어난 성과를 어떻게 인정하나요?

How does the company recognize outstanding achievements? 회사는 뛰어난 성과를 어떻게 인정하나요?

What are the common career paths in this department? 이 부서에서의 일반적인 커리어 패스는 무엇인가요?

What are the common career paths in this department? 이 부서에서의 일반적인 커리어 패스는 무엇인가요?

Can you tell me about the team I'll be joining? 제가 합류하게 될 팀에 대해 말해 줄 수 있나요?

Can you tell me about the team I'll be joining? 제가 합류하게 될 팀에 대해 말해 줄 수 있나요?

What is the typical career progression for this role? 이 역할에 대한 전형적인 커리어 진행 경로는 무엇인가요?

What is the typical career progression for this role? 이 역할에 대한 전형적인 커리어 진행 경로는 무엇인가요?

Is overtime expected in this position? 이 직위에서 초과 근무가 예상되나요?

Is overtime expected in this position? 이 직위에서 초과 근무가 예상되나요?

Shopping Excursions

Where is the nearest shopping center? - 가장 가까운 쇼핑 센터 어디에요? (Gajang gakkawoon syoping senteo eodieyo?)

Where is the nearest shopping center? - 가장 가까운 쇼핑 센터 어디에요? (Gajang gakkawoon syoping senteo eodieyo?)

How much is this shirt? - 이 셔츠 얼마에요? (I syeocheu eolmaeyo?)

How much is this shirt? - 이 셔츠 얼마에요? (I syeocheu eolmaeyo?)

Can I try on these shoes? - 이 신발 신어봐도 되나요? (I shinbal shino-bwado doena-yo?)

Can I try on these shoes? - 이 신발 신어봐도 되나요? (I shinbal shino-bwado doena-yo?)

Is there a discount on these jeans? - 이 청바지 할인 중이에요? (I cheongbaji halin jung-ieyo?)

Is there a discount on these jeans? - 이 청바지 할인 중이에요? (I cheongbaji halin jung-ieyo?)

Do you have this dress in a different size? - 이 드레스 다른 사이즈로 있나요? (I deureseu dareun saijeuro issnayo?)

Do you have this dress in a different size? - 이 드레스 다른 사이즈로 있나요? (I deureseu dareun saijeuro issnayo?)

Are there any promotions or sales happening? - 할인 행사나 프로모션이 진행 중이에요? (Halin haengsa na peulomo-sye-i jinhaeng jung-ieyo?)

Are there any promotions or sales happening? - 할인 행사나 프로모션이 진행 중이에요? (Halin haengsa na peulomo-sye-i jinhaeng jung-ieyo?)

What time does the store close today? - 오늘 가게 몇 시에 문을 닫아요? (Oneul gage myeot shie muneul dadayo?)

What time does the store close today? - 오늘 가게 몇 시에 문을 닫아요? (Oneul gage myeot shie muneul dadayo?)

I'm searching for a gift for my sister. - 여동생 선물로 찾고 있어요. (Yeodongseng seonmul-lo chajgo iss-eoyo.)

I'm searching for a gift for my sister. - 여동생 선물로 찾고 있어요. (Yeodongseng seonmul-lo chajgo iss-eoyo.)

Can I pay with a credit card? - 신용카드로 결제할 수 있어요? (Sinyongkadeulo gyeoljehal su iss-eoyo?)

Can I pay with a credit card? - 신용카드로 결제할 수 있어요? (Sinyongkadeulo gyeoljehal su iss-eoyo?)

Where is the fitting room? - 피팅 룸 어디에요? (Piting lum eodieyo?)

Where is the fitting room? - 피팅 룸 어디에요? (Piting lum eodieyo?)

Excuse me, can you help me find the accessories section? - 실례합니다, 액세서리 코너를 찾을 수 있을까요? (Sillyehamnida, aegseseori koneuleul chajeul su iss-eulkka-yo?)

Excuse me, can you help me find the accessories section? - 실례합니다, 액세서리 코너를 찾을 수 있을까요? (Sillyehamnida, aegseseori koneuleul chajeul su iss-eulkka-yo?)

I'm looking for a winter coat. - 겨울 코트를 찾고 있어요. (Gyeoul koteureul chajgo iss-eoyo.)

I'm looking for a winter coat. - 겨울 코트를 찾고 있어요. (Gyeoul koteureul chajgo iss-eoyo.)

Do you have any recommendations for stylish handbags? - 스타일리시한 핸드백을 추천해 주시겠어요? (Seutailrisihan haendeubaeg-eul chucheonhae jushigess-eoyo?)

Do you have any recommendations for stylish handbags? - 스타일리시한 핸드백을 추천해 주시겠어요? (Seutailrisihan haendeubaeg-eul chucheonhae jushigess-eoyo?)

Where can I find local designer clothing? - 현지 디자이너 의류 어디에요? (Hyeonji dijaineo uilyu eodieyo?)

Where can I find local designer clothing? - 현지 디자이너 의류 어디에요? (Hyeonji dijaineo uilyu eodieyo?)

Is there a department for children's clothing? - 아동복 코너가 있나요? (Adongbok koneuga issnayo?)

Is there a department for children's clothing? - 아동복 코너가 있나요? (Adongbok koneuga issnayo?)

Can you recommend a good store for electronics? - 전자제품을 파는 좋은 가게를 추천해 주시겠어요? (Jeonjajepum-eul paneun joh-eun gageleul chucheonhae jushigess-eoyo?)

Can you recommend a good store for electronics? - 전자제품을 파는 좋은 가게를 추천해 주시겠어요? (Jeonjajepum-eul paneun joh-eun gageleul chucheonhae jushigess-eoyo?)

Where can I find the beauty and cosmetics section? - 뷰티와 화장품 코너 어디에요? (Beauti-wa hwajangpum koneu eodieyo?)

Where can I find the beauty and cosmetics section? - 뷰티와 화장품 코너 어디에요? (Beauti-wa hwajangpum koneu eodieyo?)

I need a new laptop. Where can I find a variety of options? - 새 노트북이 필요해요. 다양한 옵션을 찾을 수 있는 곳 어디에요? (Sae noteubug-i pil-yohae-yo. Dayanghan opshon-eul chajeul su issneun got eodieyo?)

I need a new laptop. Where can I find a variety of options? - 새 노트북이 필요해요. 다양한 옵션을 찾을 수 있는 곳 어디에요? (Sae noteubug-i pil-yohae-yo. Dayanghan opshon-eul chajeul su issneun got eodieyo?)

Are there any specialty stores for sportswear? - 운동복 전문 가게가 있나요? (Undongbok jeonmun gagega issnayo?)

Are there any specialty stores for sportswear? - 운동복 전문 가게가 있나요? (Undongbok jeonmun gagega issnayo?)

Do you have a section for home decor? - 홈 데코용품을 파는 곳이 있나요? (Hom dekoyongpum-eul paneun gos-i issnayo?)

Do you have a section for home decor? - 홈 데코용품을 파는 곳이 있나요? (Hom dekoyongpum-eul paneun gos-i issnayo?)

What's the return policy for this store? - 이 가게의 교환/환불 정책이 어떻게 되나요? (I gageui gyohwan/hwanbul jeongchaeg-i eotteohge doena-yo?)

What's the return policy for this store? - 이 가게의 교환/환불 정책이 어떻게 되나요? (I gageui gyohwan/hwanbul jeongchaeg-i eotteohge doena-yo?)

Can I get a gift receipt for this purchase? - 이 구매에 대한 선물 영수증을 받을 수 있을까요? (I guma-e daehan seonmul yeongsujeung-eul badeul su iss-eulkka-yo?)

Can I get a gift receipt for this purchase? - 이 구매에 대한 선물 영수증을 받을 수 있을까요? (I guma-e daehan seonmul yeongsujeung-eul badeul su iss-eulkka-yo?)

Are there any loyalty programs or membership benefits? - 어떤 할인 프로그램이나 멤버십 혜택이 있나요? (Eotteon halin peulogeuram-ina membeoship hyetaeg-i issnayo?)

Are there any loyalty programs or membership benefits? - 어떤 할인 프로그램이나 멤버십 혜택이 있나요? (Eotteon halin peulogeuram-ina membeoship hyetaeg-i issnayo?)

Can I get this item gift-wrapped? - 이 상품을 선물포장해 주실 수 있을까요? (I sangpum-eul seonmul pojanghae jushil su iss-eulkka-yo?)

Can I get this item gift-wrapped? - 이 상품을 선물포장해 주실 수 있을까요? (I sangpum-eul seonmul pojanghae jushil su iss-eulkka-yo?)

Is there a sale or discount for local residents? - 현지 주민을 위한 할인 행사나 혜택이 있나요? (Hyeonji jumin-eul wihan halin haengsa-na hyetaeg-i issnayo?)

Is there a sale or discount for local residents? - 현지 주민을 위한 할인 행사나 혜택이 있나요? (Hyeonji jumin-eul wihan halin haengsa-na hyetaeg-i issnayo?)

Do you offer a price match guarantee? - 가격 일치 보장 서비스를 제공하나요? (Gagyeog ilchi bojang seobiseu-leul jegong-ha-na-yo?)

Do you offer a price match guarantee? - 가격 일치 보장 서비스를 제공하나요? (Gagyeog ilchi bojang seobiseu-leul jegong-ha-na-yo?)

Can I inquire about the warranty for this product? - 이 제품에 대한 보증 정보를 알 수 있을까요? (I jepum-e daehan bojeung jeongbo-reul al su iss-eulkka-yo?)

Can I inquire about the warranty for this product? - 이 제품에 대한 보증 정보를 알 수 있을까요? (I jepum-e daehan bojeung jeongbo-reul al su iss-eulkka-yo?)

Where can I find eco-friendly products? - 친환경 제품은 어디에요? (Chinhwan-gyeong jepum-eun eodieyo?)

Where can I find eco-friendly products? - 친환경 제품은 어디에요? (Chinhwan-gyeong jepum-eun eodieyo?)

Are there any ongoing promotions for loyal customers? - 충성 고객을 위한 현재 진행 중인 프로모션이 있나요? (Chungseong gogaeg-eul wihan hyeonjae jinhaeng jung-in peulomo-sye-i issnayo?)

Are there any ongoing promotions for loyal customers? - 충성 고객을 위한 현재 진행 중인 프로모션이 있나요? (Chungseong gogaeg-eul wihan hyeonjae jinhaeng jung-in peulomo-sye-i issnayo?)

I'm looking for unique and handmade items. Where should I go? - 독특하고 수공예품을 찾고 있어요. 어디로 가야 하나요? (Dokteughago sugongyepum-eul chajgo iss-eoyo. Eodilo gaya hanayo?)

I'm looking for unique and handmade items. Where should I go? - 독특하고 수공예품을 찾고 있어요. 어디로 가야 하나요? (Dokteughago sugongyepum-eul chajgo iss-eoyo. Eodilo gaya hanayo?)

Do you have a size conversion chart for international customers? - 국제 고객을 위한 사이즈 변환 차트가 있나요? (Gugje gogaeg-eul wihan saijeu byeonhwan chateu-ga issnayo?)

Do you have a size conversion chart for international customers? - 국제 고객을 위한 사이즈 변환 차트가 있나요? (Gugje gogaeg-eul wihan saijeu byeonhwan chateu-ga issnayo?)

Can you help me find the latest fashion trends? - 최신 패션 트렌드를 찾는 데 도와주세요. (Choesin paesyeon teulendeu-leul chajneun de dowajuseyo.)

Can you help me find the latest fashion trends? - 최신 패션 트렌드를 찾는 데 도와주세요. (Choesin paesyeon teulendeu-leul chajneun de dowajuseyo.)

Where can I find the best deals on electronics? - 전자제품에 대한 최고의 거래는 어디에요? (Jeonjajepum-e daehan choego-eui geolae-neun eodieyo?)

Where can I find the best deals on electronics? - 전자제품에 대한 최고의 거래는 어디에요? (Jeonjajepum-e daehan choego-eui geolae-neun eodieyo?)

I'm interested in local handmade jewelry. Where can I find it? - 현지 손으로 만든 보석에 관심이 있어요. 어디에서 찾을 수 있나요? (Hyeonji son-eulo mandeun boseog-e gwan-sim-i iss-eoyo. Eodi-eseo chajeul su issnayo?)

I'm interested in local handmade jewelry. Where can I find it? - 현지 손으로 만든 보석에 관심이 있어요. 어디에서 찾을 수 있나요? (Hyeonji son-eulo mandeun boseog-e gwan-sim-i iss-eoyo. Eodi-eseo chajeul su issnayo?)

Can I use international credit cards for payment? - 국제 신용카드로 결제할 수 있나요? (Gukje sinyongkadeulo gyeoljehal su issnayo?)

Can I use international credit cards for payment? - 국제 신용카드로 결제할 수 있나요? (Gukje sinyongkadeulo gyeoljehal su issnayo?)

Are there any restrictions on bringing purchases back to my country? - 나라로 구매물품을 가져갈 때 제약이 있나요? (Nala-ro guma-mulpum-eul gajyeo-gal ttae je-yag-i issnayo?)

Are there any restrictions on bringing purchases back to my country? - 나라로 구매물품을 가져갈 때 제약이 있나요? (Nala-ro guma-mulpum-eul gajyeo-gal ttae je-yag-i issnayo?)

I'm looking for casual wear. Where can I find a variety of options? - 캐주얼 의류를 찾고 있어요. 다양한 옵션을 찾을 수 있는 곳 어디에요?

(Kaejueol uilyu-leul chajgo iss-eoyo. Dayanghan opshon-eul chajeul su issneun got eodieyo?)

I'm looking for casual wear. Where can I find a variety of options? - 캐주얼 의류를 찾고 있어요. 다양한 옵션을 찾을 수 있는 곳 어디에요? (Kaejueol uilyu-leul chajgo iss-eoyo. Dayanghan opshon-eul chajeul su issneun got eodieyo?)

Can I get this item personalized or customized? - 이 상품을 개인화하거나 맞춤제작할 수 있을까요? (I sangpum-eul gaeinhwa hageona matchumjejaghal su iss-eulkka-yo?)

Can I get this item personalized or customized? - 이 상품을 개인화하거나 맞춤제작할 수 있을까요? (I sangpum-eul gaeinhwa hageona matchumjejaghal su iss-eulkka-yo?)

What are the popular shopping districts in the city? - 도시에서 인기 있는 쇼핑 지역은 어디에요? (Dosieseo ingi issneun syoping jiyeog-eun eodieyo?)What are the popular shopping districts in the city? - 도시에서 인기 있는 쇼핑 지역은 어디에요? (Dosieseo ingi issneun syoping jiyeog-eun eodieyo?)

Where can I find a good selection of budget-friendly items? - 저렴한 제품을 다양하게 찾을 수 있는 곳 어디에요? (Jeolyeomhan jepum-eul dayanghage chaj-eul su issneun got eodieyo?)

Where can I find a good selection of budget-friendly items? - 저렴한 제품을 다양하게 찾을 수 있는 곳 어디에요? (Jeolyeomhan jepum-eul dayanghage chaj-eul su issneun got eodieyo?)

Can you help me find stores with vintage clothing? - 빈티지 의류를 파는 가게를 찾는 데 도움을 주시겠어요? (Bintiji uilyu-leul paneun gageleul chajneun de doum-eul jusigess-eoyo?)

Can you help me find stores with vintage clothing? - 빈티지 의류를 파는 가게를 찾는 데 도움을 주시겠어요? (Bintiji uilyu-leul paneun gageleul chajneun de doum-eul jusigess-eoyo?)

Is there a separate section for local artisanal products? - 현지 예술가의 제품을 찾을 수 있는 별도의 섹션이 있나요? (Hyeonji yesulgayi jepum-eul chaj-eul su issneun byaldo-eui segsyi issnayo?)

Is there a separate section for local artisanal products? - 현지 예술가의 제품을 찾을 수 있는 별도의 섹션이 있나요? (Hyeonji yesulgayi jepum-eul chaj-eul su issneun byaldo-eui segsyi issnayo?)

Where can I find traditional Korean clothing, Hanbok? - 한복을 찾을 수 있는 곳 어디에요? (Hanbog-eul chaj-eul su issneun got eodieyo?)

Where can I find traditional Korean clothing, Hanbok? - 한복을 찾을 수 있는 곳 어디에요? (Hanbog-eul chaj-eul su issneun got eodieyo?)

Are there any duty-free shops in this area? - 이 지역에 면세점이 있나요? (I jiyeog-e myeonsejeom-i issnayo?)

Are there any duty-free shops in this area? - 이 지역에 면세점이 있나요? (I jiyeog-e myeonsejeom-i issnayo?)

Can you recommend stores with trendy accessories? - 트렌디한 액세서리를 파는 가게를 추천해 주시겠어요? (Teulendihan aegseseori-reul paneun gageleul chucheonhae jushigess-eoyo?)

Can you recommend stores with trendy accessories? - 트렌디한 액세서리를 파는 가게를 추천해 주시겠어요? (Teulendihan aegseseori-reul paneun gageleul chucheonhae jushigess-eoyo?)

Where is the nearest department store? - 가장 가까운 백화점은 어디에요?

Where is the nearest department store? - 가장 가까운 백화점은 어디에요?

How much is this shirt? - 이 셔츠는 얼마에요?

How much is this shirt? - 이 셔츠는 얼마에요?

Can I see this dress in a different size? - 이 드레스 다른 사이즈로 볼 수 있을까요?

Can I see this dress in a different size? - 이 드레스 다른 사이즈로 볼 수 있을까요?

Where can I find accessories for men? - 남성 액세서리 어디에서 찾을 수 있어요?

Where can I find accessories for men? - 남성 액세서리 어디에서 찾을 수 있어요?

Is there a sale on shoes today? - 오늘은 신발 세일이 있나요?

Is there a sale on shoes today? - 오늘은 신발 세일이 있나요?

What time does the mall close? - 쇼핑몰 몇 시에 문이 닫아요?

What time does the mall close? - 쇼핑몰 몇 시에 문이 닫아요?

I'm looking for a gift for my sister. Any suggestions? - 여동생 선물로 찾고 있어요. 어떤 걸 추천해 주세요?

I'm looking for a gift for my sister. Any suggestions? - 여동생 선물로 찾고 있어요. 어떤 걸 추천해 주세요?

Do you have this in blue? - 이건 파란색으로 있나요?

Do you have this in blue? - 이건 파란색으로 있나요?

Can I try on these jeans? - 이 청바지 입어볼 수 있을까요?

Can I try on these jeans? - 이 청바지 입어볼 수 있을까요?

Where is the cashier? - 계산대 어디에요?

Where is the cashier? - 계산대 어디에요?

Excuse me, where are the fitting rooms? - 실례합니다, 피팅 룸 어디에요?

Excuse me, where are the fitting rooms? - 실례합니다, 피팅 룸 어디에요?

Is there a discount for buying in bulk? - 대량 구매시 할인이 있나요?

Is there a discount for buying in bulk? - 대량 구매시 할인이 있나요?

Can you help me find the electronics section? - 전자제품 섹션을 찾는 데 도움을 줄 수 있나요?

Can you help me find the electronics section? - 전자제품 섹션을 찾는 데 도움을 줄 수 있나요?

Do you have a loyalty program or membership? - 회원제나 멤버십이 있나요?

Do you have a loyalty program or membership? - 회원제나 멤버십이 있나요?

I'm searching for a specific brand of perfume. - 특정 브랜드 향수 찾고 있어요.

I'm searching for a specific brand of perfume. - 특정 브랜드 향수 찾고 있어요.

Are there any special promotions today? - 오늘은 특별 프로모션이 있나요?

Are there any special promotions today? - 오늘은 특별 프로모션이 있나요?

Could you point me to the toy department? - 장난감 부문 어디에요?

Could you point me to the toy department? - 장난감 부문 어디에요?

Where can I find formal wear for weddings? - 웨딩 드레스를 찾을 수 있는 곳이 어디에요?

Where can I find formal wear for weddings? - 웨딩 드레스를 찾을 수 있는 곳이 어디에요?

Is there a restroom in this shopping center? - 이 쇼핑 센터에 화장실이 있나요?

Is there a restroom in this shopping center? - 이 쇼핑 센터에 화장실이 있나요?

Can I return items if they don't fit? - 사이즈가 맞지 않으면 반품할 수 있나요?

Can I return items if they don't fit? - 사이즈가 맞지 않으면 반품할 수 있나요?

Do you offer gift wrapping services? - 선물 포장 서비스가 있나요?

Do you offer gift wrapping services? - 선물 포장 서비스가 있나요?

Are there any eco-friendly products available? - 친환경 제품을 어디에서 찾을 수 있어요?

Are there any eco-friendly products available? - 친환경 제품을 어디에서 찾을 수 있어요?

I'm looking for a local artisan market. Any recommendations? - 지역 공예시장을 찾고 있어요. 어떤 곳이 좋아요?

I'm looking for a local artisan market. Any recommendations? - 지역 공예시장을 찾고 있어요. 어떤 곳이 좋아요?

Where is the nearest ATM? - 가장 가까운 ATM은 어디에요?

Where is the nearest ATM? - 가장 가까운 ATM은 어디에요?

Is there a lost and found in the mall? - 쇼핑몰에 분실물 보관소가 있나요?

Is there a lost and found in the mall? - 쇼핑몰에 분실물 보관소가 있나요?

Can you tell me about the return policy? - 온라인 구매에 대한 반품 정책을 알려주세요.

Can you tell me about the return policy? - 온라인 구매에 대한 반품 정책을 알려주세요.

Do you sell international SIM cards? - 국제 SIM 카드를 판매하나요?

Do you sell international SIM cards? - 국제 SIM 카드를 판매하나요?

Where can I find stylish handbags? - 세련된 핸드백 어디에서 찾을 수 있어요?

Where can I find stylish handbags? - 세련된 핸드백 어디에서 찾을 수 있어요?

What's the warranty on this appliance? - 가전제품 최소한의 보증 기간은 어떻게 되나요?

What's the warranty on this appliance? - 가전제품 최소한의 보증 기간은 어떻게 되나요?

Are there any upcoming sales events? - 다가오는 할인 행사가 있나요?

Are there any upcoming sales events? - 다가오는 할인 행사가 있나요?

I need a new pair of running shoes. Where should I look? - 새로운 운동화가 필요해요. 어디를 봐야 할까요?

I need a new pair of running shoes. Where should I look? - 새로운 운동화가 필요해요. 어디를 봐야 할까요?

Can you recommend a good bookshop in the area? - 이 지역에서 좋은 서점을 추천해 주세요?

Can you recommend a good bookshop in the area? -
이 지역에서 좋은 서점을 추천해 주세요?

Are there any pop-up shops happening soon? - 곧
열릴 팝업 샵이 있나요?

Are there any pop-up shops happening soon? - 곧
열릴 팝업 샵이 있나요?

Where is the closest grocery store? - 가장 가까운
식료품 점은 어디에요?

Where is the closest grocery store? - 가장 가까운
식료품 점은 어디에요?

Can I pay with a combination of cash and card? -
현금과 카드를 함께 사용할 수 있나요?

Can I pay with a combination of cash and card? -
현금과 카드를 함께 사용할 수 있나요?

I'm interested in buying local artwork. Any
suggestions? - 지역 아티스트가 만든 작품을 찾고
있어요. 어떤 걸 추천하세요?

I'm interested in buying local artwork. Any
suggestions? - 지역 아티스트가 만든 작품을 찾고
있어요. 어떤 걸 추천하세요?

Are there any Black Friday deals coming up? - 블랙
프라이데이 딜이 다가오나요?

Are there any Black Friday deals coming up? - 블랙
프라이데이 딜이 다가오나요?

What's the exchange policy for online purchases? - 온라인 구매에 대한 교환 정책이 어떻게 되나요?

What's the exchange policy for online purchases? - 온라인 구매에 대한 교환 정책이 어떻게 되나요?

Can I reserve this item and pay later? - 이 제품을 예약하고 나중에 결제할 수 있나요?

Can I reserve this item and pay later? - 이 제품을 예약하고 나중에 결제할 수 있나요?

Where can I find sustainable fashion brands? - 친환경 패션 브랜드를 어디에서 찾을 수 있어요?

Where can I find sustainable fashion brands? - 친환경 패션 브랜드를 어디에서 찾을 수 있어요?

Do you have any student discounts? - 학생 할인이 있나요?

Do you have any student discounts? - 학생 할인이 있나요?

Is there a sale section for clearance items? - 아울렛 상품을 위한 세일 섹션이 있나요?

Is there a sale section for clearance items? - 아울렛 상품을 위한 세일 섹션이 있나요?

Can you help me find a stylish backpack? - 세련된 백팩을 찾아주실 수 있나요?

Can you help me find a stylish backpack? - 세련된 백팩을 찾아주실 수 있나요?

Where can I find the latest tech gadgets? - 최신 테크 가전을 어디에서 찾을 수 있어요?

Where can I find the latest tech gadgets? - 최신 테크 가전을 어디에서 찾을 수 있어요?

I'm looking for a unique gift shop. Any ideas? - 독특한 선물 가게를 찾고 있어요. 어떤 곳이 좋아요?

I'm looking for a unique gift shop. Any ideas? - 독특한 선물 가게를 찾고 있어요. 어떤 곳이 좋아요?

Can I use multiple coupons on one purchase? - 하나의 구매에 여러 쿠폰을 사용할 수 있나요?

Can I use multiple coupons on one purchase? - 하나의 구매에 여러 쿠폰을 사용할 수 있나요?

What's the best time to shop for discounts? - 할인을 위한 최적의 쇼핑 시간은 언제인가요?

What's the best time to shop for discounts? - 할인을 위한 최적의 쇼핑 시간은 언제인가요?

Do you have a customer loyalty program? - 자주 쇼핑하는 손님을 위한 리워드 프로그램이 있나요?

Do you have a customer loyalty program? - 자주 쇼핑하는 손님을 위한 리워드 프로그램이 있나요?

Can you recommend a good tailor in the area? - 이 지역에서 좋은 재단을 추천해 주세요?

Can you recommend a good tailor in the area? - 이 지역에서 좋은 재단을 추천해 주세요?

Is there a discount for senior citizens? - 군인을 위한 할인이 있나요?

Is there a discount for senior citizens? - 군인을 위한 할인이 있나요?

Where can I buy organic beauty products? - 유기농 화장품을 어디에서 사볼 수 있나요?

Where can I buy organic beauty products? - 유기농 화장품을 어디에서 사볼 수 있나요?

Are there any exclusive in-store promotions? - 매장에서 독점적인 프로모션이 있나요?

Are there any exclusive in-store promotions? - 매장에서 독점적인 프로모션이 있나요?

Can you tell me where the nearest shoe store is? - 가장 가까운 신발 가게는 어디에요?

Can you tell me where the nearest shoe store is? - 가장 가까운 신발 가게는 어디에요?

What's the policy on price matching? - 가격 일치 정책은 어떻게 되나요?

What's the policy on price matching? - 가격 일치 정책은 어떻게 되나요?

I'm in search of a vintage clothing store. Any recommendations? - 빈티지 의류 가게를 찾고 있어요. 추천 좀 해주세요?

I'm in search of a vintage clothing store. Any recommendations? - 빈티지 의류 가게를 찾고 있어요. 추천 좀 해주세요?

Do you offer free shipping for online orders? - 온라인 주문에 대한 무료 배송이 가능한가요?

Do you offer free shipping for online orders? - 온라인 주문에 대한 무료 배송이 가능한가요?

Can I find local produce in this shopping district? - 이 쇼핑 지구에서 지역 농산물을 찾을 수 있나요?

Can I find local produce in this shopping district? - 이 쇼핑 지구에서 지역 농산물을 찾을 수 있나요?

Are there any art supply stores nearby? - 아트 서플라이 스토어는 어디에요?

Are there any art supply stores nearby? - 아트 서플라이 스토어는 어디에요?

Where can I buy sustainable home goods? - 친환경 가정용품을 어디에서 구매할 수 있나요?

Where can I buy sustainable home goods? - 친환경 가정용품을 어디에서 구매할 수 있나요

Can I get this item gift-wrapped? - 이 제품을 선물 포장할 수 있나요?

Can I get this item gift-wrapped? - 이 제품을 선물 포장할 수 있나요?

Is there a limit to the number of items for fitting rooms? - 피팅 룸에 아이템 수량에 제한이 있나요?

Is there a limit to the number of items for fitting rooms? - 피팅 룸에 아이템 수량에 제한이 있나요?

Can I get a rain check on this item if it's out of stock? - 이 제품이 품절이라면 나중에 언제든지 사도 될까요?

Can I get a rain check on this item if it's out of stock? - 이 제품이 품절이라면 나중에 언제든지 사도 될까요?

What's the policy on returning electronics? - 일체형 전자제품에 대한 반품 정책은 어떻게 되나요?

What's the policy on returning electronics? - 일체형 전자제품에 대한 반품 정책은 어떻게 되나요?

Do you have a rewards program for frequent shoppers? - 자주 쇼핑하는 손님을 위한 보상 프로그램이 있나요?

Do you have a rewards program for frequent shoppers? - 자주 쇼핑하는 손님을 위한 보상 프로그램이 있나요?

Where can I find pet supplies in this mall? - 이 쇼핑몰에서 애완동물 용품을 어디에서 찾을 수 있나요?

Where can I find pet supplies in this mall? - 이 쇼핑몰에서 애완동물 용품을 어디에서 찾을 수 있나요?

Can I purchase a gift card for this store? - 이 가게의 상품권을 구매할 수 있나요?

Can I purchase a gift card for this store? - 이 가게의 상품권을 구매할 수 있나요?

Are there any upcoming fashion shows or events? - 곧 열릴 패션쇼나 이벤트가 있나요?

Are there any upcoming fashion shows or events? - 곧 열릴 패션쇼나 이벤트가 있나요?

What's the policy on trying on jewelry? - 주얼리를 시착하는 데 관한 정책이 어떻게 되나요?

What's the policy on trying on jewelry? - 주얼리를 시착하는 데 관한 정책이 어떻게 되나요?

Do you have a layaway program? - 할부 제도가 있나요?

Do you have a layaway program? - 할부 제도가 있나요?

Accommodations

What is the check-in time? - 체크인 시간이 언제에요? (Chekeuin sigan-i eonjeyo?)

What is the check-in time? - 체크인 시간이 언제에요? (Chekeuin sigan-i eonjeyo?)

Is there a variety of room types? - 어떤 종류의 객실이 있나요? (Eotteon jongnyu-eui gaeksil-i issnayo?)

Is there a variety of room types? - 어떤 종류의 객실이 있나요? (Eotteon jongnyu-eui gaeksil-i issnayo?)

Is breakfast included in the room rate? - 객실 요금에 아침 식사가 포함되어 있나요? (Gaeksil yo-geum-e achim sigsaga pohamdoen-eo issnayo?)

Is breakfast included in the room rate? - 객실 요금에 아침 식사가 포함되어 있나요? (Gaeksil yo-geum-e achim sigsaga pohamdoen-eo issnayo?)

Can I request a late check-out? - 늦은 체크아웃을 요청할 수 있나요? (Neul-eun chekeu-aus-eul yocheonghal su issnayo?)

Can I request a late check-out? - 늦은 체크아웃을 요청할 수 있나요? (Neul-eun chekeu-aus-eul yocheonghal su issnayo?)

Does the room have air conditioning? - 객실에 에어컨이 있나요? (Gaeksil-e e-eokeonis issnayo?)

Does the room have air conditioning? - 객실에 에어컨이 있나요? (Gaeksil-e e-eokeonis issnayo?)

How far is the hotel from the airport? - 호텔은 공항에서 얼마나 떨어져 있나요? (Hotel-eun gonghang-eseo eolmana tteoleojyeo issnayo?)

How far is the hotel from the airport? - 호텔은 공항에서 얼마나 떨어져 있나요? (Hotel-eun gonghang-eseo eolmana tteoleojyeo issnayo?)

Are there restaurants around the hotel? - 호텔 주변에 레스토랑이 있나요? (Hotel juyeon-e leseutolang-i issnayo?)

Are there restaurants around the hotel? - 호텔 주변에 레스토랑이 있나요? (Hotel juyeon-e leseutolang-i issnayo?)

Is there a shuttle service to the city center? - 도심까지 셔틀 서비스가 있나요? (Dosimkkaji syeoteul seobiseu-ga issnayo?

Is there a shuttle service to the city center? - 도심까지 셔틀 서비스가 있나요? (Dosimkkaji syeoteul seobiseu-ga issnayo?)

I'd like a room with a good view. - 좋은 전망의 방을 예약하고 싶어요. (Joh-eun jeonmang-eui bang-eul yeyaghago sip-eoyo.)

I'd like a room with a good view. - 좋은 전망의 방을 예약하고 싶어요. (Joh-eun jeonmang-eui bang-eul yeyaghago sip-eoyo.)

Do you offer room service? - 룸 서비스를 제공하나요? (Room seobiseu-leul jegonghanayo?)

Do you offer room service? - 룸 서비스를 제공하나요? (Room seobiseu-leul jegonghanayo?)

Is parking available at the hotel? - 호텔에서 주차할 수 있나요? (Hotel-eseo jucha hal su issnayo?)

Is parking available at the hotel? - 호텔에서 주차할 수 있나요? (Hotel-eseo jucha hal su issnayo?)

I'd like a non-smoking room, please. - 비흡연 객실을 원해요. (Bihaeb-yeon gaeksil-eul wonhaeyo.)

I'd like a non-smoking room, please. - 비흡연 객실을 원해요. (Bihaeb-yeon gaeksil-eul wonhaeyo.)

Does the hotel provide local tourist information? - 호텔에서 지역 관광 정보를 제공하나요? (Hotel-eseo jieob gwangwang jeongbo-leul jegonghanayo?)

Does the hotel provide local tourist information? - 호텔에서 지역 관광 정보를 제공하나요? (Hotel-eseo jieob gwangwang jeongbo-leul jegonghanayo?)

How much is the extra bed per night? - 추가 침대는 하루에 얼마에요? (Chuga chimbang-eun halu-e eolmaeyo?)

How much is the extra bed per night? - 추가 침대는 하루에 얼마에요? (Chuga chimbang-eun halu-e eolmaeyo?)

Does the room have a refrigerator? - 방에 냉장고가 있나요? (Bang-e naengjang-go-ga issnayo?)

Does the room have a refrigerator? - 방에 냉장고가 있나요? (Bang-e naengjang-go-ga issnayo?)

Are pets allowed in the hotel? - 호텔에서 애완동물을 허용하나요? (Hotel-eseo aewandongmul-eul heoyonghanayo?)

Are pets allowed in the hotel? - 호텔에서 애완동물을 허용하나요? (Hotel-eseo aewandongmul-eul heoyonghanayo?)

How is room cleaning conducted? - 객실 청소는 어떻게 진행되나요? (Gaeksil cheongsoneun eotteohge jinhaengdoenayo?)

How is room cleaning conducted? - 객실 청소는 어떻게 진행되나요? (Gaeksil cheongsoneun eotteohge jinhaengdoenayo?)

Is there a fitness center in the hotel? - 호텔에 피트니스 센터가 있나요? (Hotel-eseo piteuniseu senteo-ga issnayo?)

Is there a fitness center in the hotel? - 호텔에 피트니스 센터가 있나요? (Hotel-eseo piteuniseu senteo-ga issnayo?)

I'd like to reserve a room for three nights. - 세 박을 예약하고 싶어요. (Se bak-eul yeyaghago sip-eoyo.)

I'd like to reserve a room for three nights. - 세 박을 예약하고 싶어요. (Se bak-eul yeyaghago sip-eoyo.)

Does the hotel offer wake-up call service? - 호텔에서 모닝콜 서비스를 제공하나요? (Hotel-eseo moningkol seobiseu-leul jegonghanayo?)

Does the hotel offer wake-up call service? - 호텔에서 모닝콜 서비스를 제공하나요? (Hotel-eseo moningkol seobiseu-leul jegonghanayo?)

What is the cancellation policy? - 취소 정책이 어떻게 되나요? (Chwiso jeongchag-i eotteohge doena-yo?)

What is the cancellation policy? - 취소 정책이 어떻게 되나요? (Chwiso jeongchag-i eotteohge doena-yo?)

Can the swimming pool be used for free? - 수영장은 무료로 이용할 수 있나요? (Suyeongjang-eun mulolyo iyonghal su issnayo?)

Can the swimming pool be used for free? - 수영장은 무료로 이용할 수 있나요? (Suyeongjang-eun mulolyo iyonghal su issnayo?)

Can I have a room with an ocean view? - 바다가 보이는 방을 원해요. (Bada-ga boineun bang-eul wonhaeyo.)

Can I have a room with an ocean view? - 바다가 보이는 방을 원해요. (Bada-ga boineun bang-eul wonhaeyo.)

Is there a lounge in the hotel? - 호텔에 라운지가 있나요? (Hotel-eseo raunji-ga issnayo?)

Is there a lounge in the hotel? - 호텔에 라운지가 있나요? (Hotel-eseo raunji-ga issnayo?)

What is the Wi-Fi password? - Wi-Fi 비밀번호는 뭐에요? (Wi-Fi bimilbeonhoneyo?)

What is the Wi-Fi password? - Wi-Fi 비밀번호는 뭐에요? (Wi-Fi bimilbeonhoneyo?)

Can you send a reservation confirmation email? - 예약 확인 이메일을 보낼 수 있을까요? (Yeyag hwagin imeil-eul bonael su iss-eulkka-yo?)

Can you send a reservation confirmation email? - 예약 확인 이메일을 보낼 수 있을까요? (Yeyag hwagin imeil-eul bonael su iss-eulkka-yo?)

Are there any nearby attractions or landmarks? - 근처에 볼 만한 곳이나 명소가 있나요? (Geuncheo-e bol manhan got-ina myeongso-ga issnayo?)

Are there any nearby attractions or landmarks? - 근처에 볼 만한 곳이나 명소가 있나요? (Geuncheo-e bol manhan got-ina myeongso-ga issnayo?)

Can I order meals through room service? - 룸 서비스로 식사를 주문할 수 있나요? (Room seobiseu-lo sigsa-reul jumunhal su issnayo?)

Can I order meals through room service? - 룸 서비스로 식사를 주문할 수 있나요? (Room seobiseu-lo sigsa-reul jumunhal su issnayo?)

I have a reservation under the name [Your Name]. - 제 이름으로 예약한 건데요. ([Your Name]-euro yeyaghan geondedo.)

I have a reservation under the name [Your Name]. - 제 이름으로 예약한 건데요. ([Your Name]-euro yeyaghan geondedo.)

Can I rent bicycles from the hotel? - 호텔에서 자전거 대여 서비스가 있나요? (Hotel-eseo jajeongeo daelyeo seobiseu-ga issnayo?)

Can I rent bicycles from the hotel? - 호텔에서 자전거 대여 서비스가 있나요? (Hotel-eseo jajeongeo daelyeo seobiseu-ga issnayo?)

How are lost and found items handled? - 분실물은 어떻게 처리되나요? (Bunsilmul-eun eotteohge chulihdoenayo?)

How are lost and found items handled? - 분실물은 어떻게 처리되나요? (Bunsilmul-eun eotteohge chulihdoenayo?)

Can I request a wake-up call? - 모닝콜을 요청할 수 있나요? (Moningkol-eul yocheonghal su issnayo?)

Can I request a wake-up call? - 모닝콜을 요청할 수 있나요? (Moningkol-eul yocheonghal su issnayo?)

Can I use the hotel's meeting room? - 호텔에서 회의실을 이용할 수 있나요? (Hotel-eseo hoeuisil-eul iyonghal su issnayo?)

Can I use the hotel's meeting room? - 호텔에서 회의실을 이용할 수 있나요? (Hotel-eseo hoeuisil-eul iyonghal su issnayo?)

Is there a safe in the room? - 방에 금고가 있나요? (Bang-e geumgo-ga issnayo?)

Is there a safe in the room? - 방에 금고가 있나요? (Bang-e geumgo-ga issnayo?)

Does the room have a refrigerator? - 방에 냉장고가 있나요? (Bang-e naengjang-go-ga issnayo?)

Does the room have a refrigerator? - 방에 냉장고가 있나요? (Bang-e naengjang-go-ga issnayo?)

Can I leave my luggage after check-out? - 체크아웃 후에도 짐을 보관할 수 있나요? (Chekeu-aus hu-e-do jim-eul bogwanhal su issnayo?)

Can I leave my luggage after check-out? - 체크아웃 후에도 짐을 보관할 수 있나요? (Chekeu-aus hu-e-do jim-eul bogwanhal su issnayo?)

I'd like a room with twin beds, please. - 쌍둥이 침대가 있는 방으로 부탁해요. (Ssangdung-i chimbang-a issneun bang-eulo butaghaeyo.)

I'd like a room with twin beds, please. - 쌍둥이 침대가 있는 방으로 부탁해요. (Ssangdung-i chimbang-a issneun bang-eulo butaghaeyo.)

Does the hotel provide childcare services? - 호텔에서 어린이 돌봄 서비스를 제공하나요? (Hotel-eseo eolin-i dolbom seobiseu-leul jegonghanayo?)

Does the hotel provide childcare services? - 호텔에서 어린이 돌봄 서비스를 제공하나요? (Hotel-eseo eolin-i dolbom seobiseu-leul jegonghanayo?)

What is the policy for early check-in? - 일찍 체크인하는 데 어떤 정책이 있나요? (Iljjig chekeuin-haneun de eotteon jeongchag-i issnayo?)

What is the policy for early check-in? - 일찍 체크인하는 데 어떤 정책이 있나요? (Iljjig chekeuin-haneun de eotteon jeongchag-i issnayo?)

Does the room have a hairdryer? - 방에 헤어 드라이어가 있나요? (Bang-e heeo deuraieoga issnayo?)

Does the room have a hairdryer? - 방에 헤어 드라이어가 있나요? (Bang-e heeo deuraieoga issnayo?)

Can I have a wake-up call at 7 AM tomorrow? - 내일 아침 7시에 모닝콜 받을 수 있을까요?

(Nae-il achim 7si-e moningkol badeul su
iss-eulkka-yo?)

Can I have a wake-up call at 7 AM tomorrow? -
내일 아침 7시에 모닝콜 받을 수 있을까요?
(Nae-il achim 7si-e moningkol badeul su
iss-eulkka-yo?)

Does the hotel provide complimentary breakfast? -
호텔에서 무료 아침 식사를 제공하나요?
(Hotel-eseo mulo achim sigsa-leul jegonghanayo?)

Does the hotel provide complimentary breakfast? -
호텔에서 무료 아침 식사를 제공하나요?
(Hotel-eseo mulo achim sigsa-leul jegonghanayo?)

What amenities are included in the room? - 방에는
어떤 편의 시설들이 포함되어 있나요?
(Bang-e-neun eotteon pyeonui siseul-deul-i
pohamdoen-eo issnayo?)

What amenities are included in the room? - 방에는
어떤 편의 시설들이 포함되어 있나요?
(Bang-e-neun eotteon pyeonui siseul-deul-i
pohamdoen-eo issnayo?)

Can I use the hotel's shuttle service? - 호텔에서
제공하는 셔틀 서비스를 이용할 수 있나요?
(Hotel-eseo jegonghaneun syeoteul seobiseu-leul
iyonghal su issnayo?)

Can I use the hotel's shuttle service? - 호텔에서
제공하는 셔틀 서비스를 이용할 수 있나요?

(Hotel-eseo jegonghaneun syeoteul seobiseu-leul iyonghal su issnayo?)

I'd like to extend my stay for one more night. - 하루 더 머무르고 싶어요. (Halu deo meomuleugo sip-eoyo.)

I'd like to extend my stay for one more night. - 하루 더 머무르고 싶어요. (Halu deo meomuleugo sip-eoyo.)

Does the hotel offer laundry services? - 호텔에서 세탁 서비스를 제공하나요? (Hotel-eseo setag seobiseu-leul jegonghanayo?)

Does the hotel offer laundry services? - 호텔에서 세탁 서비스를 제공하나요? (Hotel-eseo setag seobiseu-leul jegonghanayo?)

Can I have a room on a higher floor? - 높은 층의 방을 얻을 수 있나요? (Nop-eun chung-ui bang-eul eod-eul su issnayo?)

Can I have a room on a higher floor? - 높은 층의 방을 얻을 수 있나요? (Nop-eun chung-ui bang-eul eod-eul su issnayo?)

What's the policy on bringing outside food? - 외부 음식을 가져오는 데 어떤 정책이 있나요? (Oebu eumsig-eul gajyeo-oneun de eotteon jeongchag-i issnayo?)

What's the policy on bringing outside food? - 외부 음식을 가져오는 데 어떤 정책이 있나요? (Oebu eumsig-eul gajyeo-oneun de eotteon jeongchag-i issnayo?)

Does the hotel provide airport shuttle service? - 호텔에서 공항 셔틀 서비스를 제공하나요? (Hotel-eseo gonghang syeoteul seobiseu-leul jegonghanayo?)

Does the hotel provide airport shuttle service? - 호텔에서 공항 셔틀 서비스를 제공하나요? (Hotel-eseo gonghang syeoteul seobiseu-leul jegonghanayo?)

How do I connect to the Wi-Fi in the room? - 방 안에서 Wi-Fi에 어떻게 연결하나요? (Bang an-eseo Wi-Fi-e eotteohge yeonculh-anayo?)

How do I connect to the Wi-Fi in the room? - 방 안에서 Wi-Fi에 어떻게 연결하나요? (Bang an-eseo Wi-Fi-e eotteohge yeonculh-anayo?)

Can the hotel host weddings? - 호텔에서 결혼식을 열 수 있나요? (Hotel-eseo gyeolhonsig-eul yeol su issnayo?)

Can the hotel host weddings? - 호텔에서 결혼식을 열 수 있나요? (Hotel-eseo gyeolhonsig-eul yeol su issnayo?)

Can I change the reservation dates? - 예약 날짜를 변경할 수 있나요? (Yeyag naljaleul byeongyeonghal su issnayo?)

Can I change the reservation dates? - 예약 날짜를 변경할 수 있나요? (Yeyag naljaleul byeongyeonghal su issnayo?)

Can children use the hotel's pool? - 호텔에서 어린이들이 수영장을 이용할 수 있나요? (Hotel-eseo eolin-i-deul-i suyeongjang-eul iyonghal su issnayo?)

Can children use the hotel's pool? - 호텔에서 어린이들이 수영장을 이용할 수 있나요? (Hotel-eseo eolin-i-deul-i suyeongjang-eul iyonghal su issnayo?)

Is there a dress code for the hotel restaurant? - 호텔 레스토랑에 들어갈 때 드레스 코드가 있나요? (Hotel leseutolang-e deul-eogal ttae deuleseu kodeu-ga issnayo?)

Is there a dress code for the hotel restaurant? - 호텔 레스토랑에 들어갈 때 드레스 코드가 있나요? (Hotel leseutolang-e deul-eogal ttae deuleseu kodeu-ga issnayo?)

How do I get to [Landmark] from the hotel? - 호텔에서 [랜드마크]로 어떻게 가나요? (Hotel-eseo [Laendeumakeu]-lo eotteohge gana-yo?)

How do I get to [Landmark] from the hotel? - 호텔에서 [랜드마크]로 어떻게 가나요? (Hotel-eseo [Laendeumakeu]-lo eotteohge gana-yo?)

Does the hotel have a business center? - 호텔에 비즈니스 센터가 있나요? (Hotel-eseo bizeuniseu senteo-ga issnayo?)

Does the hotel have a business center? - 호텔에 비즈니스 센터가 있나요? (Hotel-eseo bizeuniseu senteo-ga issnayo?)

Can non-guests use the gym? - 호텔 체육관을 이용하지 않는 사람들도 사용할 수 있나요? (Hotel cheyukgwan-eul iyonghaji anhneun salamdeul-do sayonghal su issnayo?)

Can non-guests use the gym? - 호텔 체육관을 이용하지 않는 사람들도 사용할 수 있나요? (Hotel cheyukgwan-eul iyonghaji anhneun salamdeul-do sayonghal su issnayo?)

Does the hotel provide car rental services? - 호텔에서 자동차 대여 서비스를 제공하나요? (Hotel-eseo jadongcha daelyeo seobiseu-leul jegonghanayo?)

Does the hotel provide car rental services? - 호텔에서 자동차 대여 서비스를 제공하나요? (Hotel-eseo jadongcha daelyeo seobiseu-leul jegonghanayo?)

Are there any nearby convenience stores? - 근처에 편의점이 있나요? (Geuncheo-e pyeonuijeom-i issnayo?)

Are there any nearby convenience stores? - 근처에 편의점이 있나요? (Geuncheo-e pyeonuijeom-i issnayo?)

Is there a minibar in the room? - 방에 미니바가 있나요? (Bang-e minibaga issnayo?)

Is there a minibar in the room? - 방에 미니바가 있나요? (Bang-e minibaga issnayo?)

Can guests use the sauna? - 손님들은 사우나를 이용할 수 있나요? (Sonnim-deul-eun sauna-leul iyonghal su issnayo?)

Can guests use the sauna? - 손님들은 사우나를 이용할 수 있나요? (Sonnim-deul-eun sauna-leul iyonghal su issnayo?)

Emergency Situations:

I've been in an accident. - 사고가 났어요. (Sagoga natseoyo.)

I've been in an accident. - 사고가 났어요. (Sagoga natseoyo.)

Where is the police station? - 경찰서 어디에요? (Gyeongchalseo eodi-eyo?)

Where is the police station? - 경찰서 어디에요? (Gyeongchalseo eodi-eyo?)

There's a fire in the building. - 건물에 불이 났어요. (Geonmul-e bul-i natseoyo.)

There's a fire in the building. - 건물에 불이 났어요. (Geonmul-e bul-i natseoyo.)

My friend needs help. - 제 친구가 도움이 필요해요. (Je chinguga doumi pil-yohae-yo.)

My friend needs help. - 제 친구가 도움이 필요해요. (Je chinguga doumi pil-yohae-yo.)

I'm feeling dizzy. - 현기증이 나요. (Hyeongijeungi nayo.)

I'm feeling dizzy. - 현기증이 나요. (Hyeongijeungi nayo.)

Please, call for help. - 도와줄 수 있는 사람을 부르세요. (Dowajul su issneun saram-eul buleuseyo.)

Please, call for help. - 도와줄 수 있는 사람을 부르세요. (Dowajul su issneun saram-eul buleuseyo.)

I've lost my wallet. - 지갑을 잃어버렸어요. (Jigab-eul ilheobeoryeosseoyo.)

I've lost my wallet. - 지갑을 잃어버렸어요. (Jigab-eul ilheobeoryeosseoyo.)

Where is the nearest pharmacy? - 가장 가까운 약국 어디에요? (Gajang gakkao-un yakguk eodi-eyo?)

Where is the nearest pharmacy? - 가장 가까운 약국 어디에요? (Gajang gakkao-un yakguk eodi-eyo?)

I can't find my way back. - 돌아갈 길을 찾을 수 없어요. (Dolagal gil-eul chajeul su eobs-eoyo.)

I can't find my way back. - 돌아갈 길을 찾을 수 없어요. (Dolagal gil-eul chajeul su eobs-eoyo.)

There's a suspicious person. - 수상한 사람이 있어요. (Susanghan saram-i iss-eoyo.)

There's a suspicious person. - 수상한 사람이 있어요. (Susanghan saram-i iss-eoyo.)

I'm having difficulty breathing. - 숨쉬기 어려워요. (Sumswig-i eolyeowo-yo.)

I'm having difficulty breathing. - 숨쉬기 어려워요. (Sumswig-i eolyeowo-yo.)

I need help translating. - 번역 도와주세요. (Beonyeok dowajuseyo.)

I need help translating. - 번역 도와주세요. (Beonyeok dowajuseyo.)

I'm feeling extremely cold. - 추워 죽겠어요. (Chuwo jukgesseoyo.)

I'm feeling extremely cold. - 추워 죽겠어요. (Chuwo jukgesseoyo.)

I'm trapped. - 갇혀 있어요. (Gathyeo iss-eoyo.)

I'm trapped. - 갇혀 있어요. (Gathyeo iss-eoyo.)

I've been bitten by something. - 뭔가에 물렸어요. (Mwonga-e mollyeosseoyo.)

I've been bitten by something. - 뭔가에 물렸어요. (Mwonga-e mollyeosseoyo.)

There's been a power outage. - 전기가 나갔어요. (Jeongiga nagass-eoyo.)

There's been a power outage. - 전기가 나갔어요. (Jeongiga nagass-eoyo.)

I need legal assistance. - 법적 도움이 필요해요. (Beobjeog doumi pil-yohae-yo.)

I need legal assistance. - 법적 도움이 필요해요. (Beobjeog doumi pil-yohae-yo.)

I've lost my child. - 제 아이를 잃어버렸어요. (Je ai-reul ilheobeoryeosseoyo.)

I've lost my child. - 제 아이를 잃어버렸어요. (Je ai-reul ilheobeoryeosseoyo.)

I see smoke. - 연기가 보여요. (Yeongiga boyeoyo.)

I see smoke. - 연기가 보여요. (Yeongiga boyeoyo.)

Please stay with me. - 나와 함께 있어주세요. (Nawa hamkke iss-eo juseyo.)

Please stay with me. - 나와 함께 있어주세요. (Nawa hamkke iss-eo juseyo.)

I'm feeling extremely hot. - 더워 죽겠어요. (Deowo jukgesseoyo.)

I'm feeling extremely hot. - 더워 죽겠어요. (Deowo jukgesseoyo.)

My phone is not working. - 핸드폰이 고장났어요. (Haendeupon-i gojangnasseoyo.)

My phone is not working. - 핸드폰이 고장났어요. (Haendeupon-i gojangnasseoyo.)

I need food and water. - 음식과 물이 필요해요. (Eumsik-gwa mul-i pil-yohae-yo.)

I need food and water. - 음식과 물이 필요해요. (Eumsik-gwa mul-i pil-yohae-yo.)

Please help me find my family. - 제 가족을 찾아주십시오. (Je gajog-eul chaj-ajusibsio.)

Please help me find my family. - 제 가족을 찾아주십시오. (Je gajog-eul chaj-ajusibsio.)

There's been a car accident. - 차가 충돌했어요. (Chaga chungdolhaesseoyo.)

There's been a car accident. - 차가 충돌했어요. (Chaga chungdolhaesseoyo.)

I feel like I'm going to faint. - 쓰러질 것 같아요. (Sseoleojil geos gatayo.)

I feel like I'm going to faint. - 쓰러질 것 같아요. (Sseoleojil geos gatayo.)

I need shelter. - 대피할 곳이 필요해요. (Daepihal gos-i pil-yohae-yo.)

I need shelter. - 대피할 곳이 필요해요. (Daepihal gos-i pil-yohae-yo.)

I'm being followed. - 나를 따라오고 있어요. (Naleul ttalaogo iss-eoyo.)

I'm being followed. - 나를 따라오고 있어요. (Naleul ttalaogo iss-eoyo.)

I can't find my way home. - 집에 돌아갈 길을 찾을 수 없어요. (Jib-e dol-agal gil-eul chaj-eul su eobs-eoyo.)

I can't find my way home. - 집에 돌아갈 길을 찾을 수 없어요. (Jib-e dol-agal gil-eul chaj-eul su eobs-eoyo.)

There's been a theft. - 도난이 있었어요. (Donan-i iss-eosseoyo.)

There's been a theft. - 도난이 있었어요. (Donan-i iss-eosseoyo.)

I need assistance with translation. - 번역 도움이 필요해요. (Beonyeok doumi pil-yohae-yo.)

I need assistance with translation. - 번역 도움이 필요해요. (Beonyeok doumi pil-yohae-yo.)

I'm feeling nauseous. - 메스꺼워요. (Meskkeowoyo.)

I'm feeling nauseous. - 메스꺼워요. (Meskkeowoyo.)

I'm feeling weak. - 힘이 없어요. (Him-i eobs-eoyo.)

I'm feeling weak. - 힘이 없어요. (Him-i eobs-eoyo.)

I can't find my keys. - 열쇠를 찾을 수 없어요. (Yeolsoeleul chaj-eul su eobs-eoyo.)

I can't find my keys. - 열쇠를 찾을 수 없어요. (Yeolsoeleul chaj-eul su eobs-eoyo.)

Please call for help. - 도움을 부르세요. (Doumeul buleuseyo.)

Please call for help. - 도움을 부르세요. (Doumeul buleuseyo.)

I'm lost in the city. - 도시에서 길을 잃었어요. (Dosieseo gil-eul ilheosseoyo.)

I'm lost in the city. - 도시에서 길을 잃었어요. (Dosieseo gil-eul ilheosseoyo.)

There's a gas leak. - 가스가 샐어 나와요. (Gaseu-ga sael-eo nawayo.)

There's a gas leak. - 가스가 샐어 나와요. (Gaseu-ga sael-eo nawayo.)

I need a doctor. - 의사가 필요해요. (Uisaga pil-yohae-yo.)

I need a doctor. - 의사가 필요해요. (Uisaga pil-yohae-yo.)

Please help me find my friends. - 제 친구들을 찾아주십시오. (Je chingudeul-eul chaj-ajusibsio.)

Please help me find my friends. - 제 친구들을 찾아주십시오. (Je chingudeul-eul chaj-ajusibsio.)

I'm feeling numb. - 무감각해져 가요. (Mugamgakhaejyeo gayo.)

I'm feeling numb. - 무감각해져 가요. (Mugamgakhaejyeo gayo.)

There's been a natural disaster. - 자연 재해가 있었어요. (Jayeon jaehae-ga iss-eosseoyo.)

There's been a natural disaster. - 자연 재해가 있었어요. (Jayeon jaehae-ga iss-eosseoyo.)

I'm having chest pain. - 가슴이 아파와요. (Gaseum-i apa-wayo.)

I'm having chest pain. - 가슴이 아파와요. (Gaseum-i apa-wayo.)

Please, stay calm. - 차분히 계세요. (Chabunhi gyeseyo.)

Please, stay calm. - 차분히 계세요. (Chabunhi gyeseyo.)

I'm feeling disoriented. - 방향을 잃었어요. (Banghyang-eul ilheosseoyo.)

I'm feeling disoriented. - 방향을 잃었어요. (Banghyang-eul ilheosseoyo.)

I'm stranded. - 막혀 있어요. (Makhyeo iss-eoyo.)

I'm stranded. - 막혀 있어요. (Makhyeo iss-eoyo.)

There's been a flood. - 홍수가 나왔어요. (Hongsu-ga nawass-eoyo.)

There's been a flood. - 홍수가 나왔어요.
(Hongsu-ga nawass-eoyo.)

I'm feeling extremely anxious. - 초조해 죽겠어요.
(Chojohae jukgesseoyo.)

I'm feeling extremely anxious. - 초조해 죽겠어요.
(Chojohae jukgesseoyo.)

I need to report a crime. - 범죄를 신고해야 해요.
(Beomjoeleul singohae-ya haeyo.)

I need to report a crime. - 범죄를 신고해야 해요.
(Beomjoeleul singohae-ya haeyo.)

I'm stuck in an elevator. - 엘리베이터에
갇혀 있어요. (Ellibeiteo-e gathyeo iss-eoyo.)

I'm stuck in an elevator. - 엘리베이터에
갇혀 있어요. (Ellibeiteo-e gathyeo iss-eoyo.)

Please, help me find my pet. - 제 반려동물을
찾아주세요. (Je ballyeodongmul-eul chaj-ajuseyo.)

Please, help me find my pet. - 제 반려동물을
찾아주세요. (Je ballyeodongmul-eul chaj-ajuseyo.)

I'm feeling lightheaded. - 머리가 어지러와요.
(Meoliga eojileowayo.)

I'm feeling lightheaded. - 머리가 어지러와요.
(Meoliga eojileowayo.)

There's been an earthquake. - 지진이 있었어요.
(Jijin-i iss-eosseoyo.)

There's been an earthquake. - 지진이 있었어요. (Jijin-i iss-eosseoyo.)

I need to contact my embassy. - 대사관에 연락해야 해요. (Daesagwan-e yeonlaghaeya haeyo.)

I need to contact my embassy. - 대사관에 연락해야 해요. (Daesagwan-e yeonlaghaeya haeyo.)

I'm having trouble speaking. - 말하기가 힘들어져요. (Malhagiga himdeuleojyeoyo.)

I'm having trouble speaking. - 말하기가 힘들어져요. (Malhagiga himdeuleojyeoyo.)

I'm feeling overwhelmed. - 너무 힘들어요. (Neomu himdeuleoyo.)

I'm feeling overwhelmed. - 너무 힘들어요. (Neomu himdeuleoyo.)

I need a place to stay. - 머물 곳이 필요해요. (Meomun gos-i pil-yohae-yo.)

I need a place to stay. - 머물 곳이 필요해요. (Meomun gos-i pil-yohae-yo.)

I can't find my glasses. - 안경을 찾을 수 없어요. (Angyeong-eul chaj-eul su eobs-eoyo.)

I can't find my glasses. - 안경을 찾을 수 없어요. (Angyeong-eul chaj-eul su eobs-eoyo.)

I need assistance with communication. - 의사소통 도움이 필요해요. (Uisaso-tong doumi pil-yohae-yo.)

I need assistance with communication. - 의사소통
도움이 필요해요. (Uisaso-tong doumi
pil-yohae-yo.)

There's been a chemical spill. - 화학 물질 유출이
있었어요. (Hwahag muljil yuchul-i iss-eosseoyo.)

There's been a chemical spill. - 화학 물질 유출이
있었어요. (Hwahag muljil yuchul-i iss-eosseoyo.)

I need to find a translator. - 번역사를 찾아야 해요.
(Beonyeogsa-reul chaj-aya haeyo.)

I need to find a translator. - 번역사를 찾아야 해요.
(Beonyeogsa-reul chaj-aya haeyo.)

I'm feeling claustrophobic. - 비행기 안에서
답답해져요. (Bihaenggi an-eseo dapdaphaejyeoyo.)

I'm feeling claustrophobic. - 비행기 안에서
답답해져요. (Bihaenggi an-eseo dapdaphaejyeoyo.)

I need help with transportation. - 교통 수단 도움이
필요해요. (Gyotong sudan doumi pil-yohae-yo.)

I need help with transportation. - 교통 수단 도움이
필요해요. (Gyotong sudan doumi pil-yohae-yo.)

I'm having trouble seeing. - 보이기가 힘들어져요.
(Boigiga himdeuleojyeoyo.)

I'm having trouble seeing. - 보이기가 힘들어져요.
(Boigiga himdeuleojyeoyo.)

There's been a gas explosion. - 가스 폭발이
있었어요. (Gaseu pogbal-i iss-eosseoyo.)

There's been a gas explosion. - 가스 폭발이 있었어요. (Gaseu pogbal-i iss-eosseoyo.)

I need help with navigation. - 길 안내 도움이 필요해요. (Gil annae doumi pil-yohae-yo.)

I need help with navigation. - 길 안내 도움이 필요해요. (Gil annae doumi pil-yohae-yo.)

I'm feeling agitated. - 동요해져 가요. (Dongyohaejyeo gayo.)

I'm feeling agitated. - 동요해져 가요. (Dongyohaejyeo gayo.)

I'm in danger. - 위험해요. (Wiheomhaeyo.)

I'm in danger. - 위험해요. (Wiheomhaeyo.)

I need help with my vehicle. - 차량 수리 도움이 필요해요. (Chal-lyang sul-i doumi pil-yohae-yo.)

I need help with my vehicle. - 차량 수리 도움이 필요해요. (Chal-lyang sul-i doumi pil-yohae-yo.)

I'm feeling feverish. - 열이 나요. (Yeol-i nayo.)

I'm feeling feverish. - 열이 나요. (Yeol-i nayo.)

There's been a terrorist attack. - 테러 공격이 있었어요. (Tereu gong-gyeok-i iss-eosseoyo.)

There's been a terrorist attack. - 테러 공격이 있었어요. (Tereu gong-gyeok-i iss-eosseoyo.)

I need assistance with communication. - 의사소통 도움이 필요해요. (Uisaso-tong doumi pil-yohae-yo.)

I need assistance with communication. - 의사소통 도움이 필요해요. (Uisaso-tong doumi pil-yohae-yo.)

I'm feeling dehydrated. - 탈수증상이 나타나요. (Talsu jeungsang-i natanayo.)

I'm feeling dehydrated. - 탈수증상이 나타나요. (Talsu jeungsang-i natanayo.)

I need help with my computer. - 컴퓨터 수리 도움이 필요해요. (Keompyuteo sul-i doumi pil-yohae-yo.)

I need help with my computer. - 컴퓨터 수리 도움이 필요해요. (Keompyuteo sul-i doumi pil-yohae-yo.)

I can't find my way out. - 나갈 길을 찾을 수 없어요. (Nagal gil-eul chaj-eul su eobs-eoyo.)

I can't find my way out. - 나갈 길을 찾을 수 없어요. (Nagal gil-eul chaj-eul su eobs-eoyo.)

There's been a hostage situation. - 인질 상황이 있었어요. (Injil sanghwang-i iss-eosseoyo.)

There's been a hostage situation. - 인질 상황이 있었어요. (Injil sanghwang-i iss-eosseoyo.)

I need help with my luggage. - 짐 처리 도움이 필요해요. (Jim cheoli doumi pil-yohae-yo.)

I need help with my luggage. - 짐 처리 도움이 필요해요. (Jim cheoli doumi pil-yohae-yo.)

I'm feeling overwhelmed. - 너무 힘들어요. (Neomu himdeuleoyo.)

I'm feeling overwhelmed. - 너무 힘들어요. (Neomu himdeuleoyo.)

I need help with my finances. - 재정 도움이 필요해요. (Jaejeong doumi pil-yohae-yo.)

I need help with my finances. - 재정 도움이 필요해요. (Jaejeong doumi pil-yohae-yo.)

I'm feeling anxious. - 불안해져 가요. (Buranhaejyeo gayo.)

I'm feeling anxious. - 불안해져 가요. (Buranhaejyeo gayo.)

I need assistance with technology. - 기술 도움이 필요해요. (Gisul doumi pil-yohae-yo.)

I need assistance with technology. - 기술 도움이 필요해요. (Gisul doumi pil-yohae-yo.)

I'm feeling faint. - 실신할 것 같아요. (Silsinhal geos gatayo.)

I'm feeling faint. - 실신할 것 같아요. (Silsinhal geos gatayo.)

I need help with my documents. - 서류 처리 도움이 필요해요. (Seolyu cheoli doumi pil-yohae-yo.)

I need help with my documents. - 서류 처리 도움이 필요해요. (Seolyu cheoli doumi pil-yohae-yo.)

I'm feeling overwhelmed. - 너무 힘들어요. (Neomu himdeuleoyo.)

I'm feeling overwhelmed. - 너무 힘들어요. (Neomu himdeuleoyo.)

I need help with my phone. - 핸드폰 수리 도움이 필요해요. (Haendeupon sul-i doumi pil-yohae-yo.)

I need help with my phone. - 핸드폰 수리 도움이 필요해요. (Haendeupon sul-i doumi pil-yohae-yo.)

Help! - 도와주세요! (Dowajuseyo!)

Help! - 도와주세요! (Dowajuseyo!)

Call the police! - 경찰을 호출하세요! (Gyeongchal-eul hohwas haseyo!)

Call the police! - 경찰을 호출하세요! (Gyeongchal-eul hohwas haseyo!)

I need an ambulance. - 구급차가 필요해요. (Gu-geubcha-ga pil-yo-hae-yo.)

I need an ambulance. - 구급차가 필요해요. (Gu-geubcha-ga pil-yo-hae-yo.)

Where is the nearest hospital? - 가장 가까운 병원 어디에요? (Gajang gakkao-un byeongwon eodi-eyo?)

Where is the nearest hospital? - 가장 가까운 병원 어디에요? (Gajang gakkao-un byeongwon eodi-eyo?)

I'm injured. - 다쳤어요. (Dachyeosseoyo.)

I'm injured. - 다쳤어요. (Dachyeosseoyo.)

Fire! - 불이 났어요! (Bul-i nasseoyo!)

Fire! - 불이 났어요! (Bul-i nasseoyo!)

I'm lost. - 길을 잃었어요. (Gireul ilheosseoyo.)

I'm lost. - 길을 잃었어요. (Gireul ilheosseoyo.)

I can't find my belongings. - 물건을 찾을 수 없어요. (Mulgeon-eul chajeul su eobs-eoyo.)

I can't find my belongings. - 물건을 찾을 수 없어요. (Mulgeon-eul chajeul su eobs-eoyo.)

I'm feeling unwell. - 몸이 안 좋아요. (Momi an johayo.)

I'm feeling unwell. - 몸이 안 좋아요. (Momi an johayo.)

I've been robbed. - 강도에게 당했어요. (Gangdo-ege danghaesseoyo.)

I've been robbed. - 강도에게 당했어요. (Gangdo-ege danghaesseoyo.)

I can't breathe. - 숨을 못 쉬겠어요. (Sum-eul mot swigesseoyo.)

I can't breathe. - 숨을 못 쉬겠어요. (Sum-eul mot swigesseoyo.)

I lost my passport. - 여권을 잃어버렸어요. (Yeogwon-eul ilheobeoryeosseoyo.)

I lost my passport. - 여권을 잃어버렸어요. (Yeogwon-eul ilheobeoryeosseoyo.)

Someone is following me. - 누군가 나를 따라와요. (Nugunga naleul ttarawayo.)

Someone is following me. - 누군가 나를 따라와요. (Nugunga naleul ttarawayo.)

My car broke down. - 차가 고장 났어요. (Chaga gojang nasseoyo.)

My car broke down. - 차가 고장 났어요. (Chaga gojang nasseoyo.)

I'm allergic to... - ...에 알레르기가 있어요. (...e alleeogiga iss-eoyo.)

I'm allergic to... - ...에 알레르기가 있어요. (...e alleeogiga iss-eoyo.)

At the Airport:

Excuse me, where is the check-in counter? 신고서 표시대는 어디에요? (Shingoseo pyosidaeneun eodieyo?)

Excuse me, where is the check-in counter? 신고서 표시대는 어디에요? (Shingoseo pyosidaeneun eodieyo?)

I have a reservation. 예약했어요. (Yeyakhaesseoyo.)

I have a reservation. 예약했어요. (Yeyakhaesseoyo.)

What time is my flight to Seoul? 서울행 비행기는 몇 시에요? (Seoulhaeng bihaenggineun myeot sieyo?)

What time is my flight to Seoul? 서울행 비행기는 몇 시에요? (Seoulhaeng bihaenggineun myeot sieyo?)

Where is the baggage claim? 수하물 수령대는 어디에요? (Suhamul sureongdaeneun eodieyo?)

Where is the baggage claim? 수하물 수령대는 어디에요? (Suhamul sureongdaeneun eodieyo?)

Is there a shuttle to the city center? 시내행 셔틀이 있나요? (Sinaehaeng syeoteul-i issnayo?)

Is there a shuttle to the city center? 시내행 셔틀이 있나요? (Sinaehaeng syeoteul-i issnayo?)

Can I get a taxi here? 여기서 택시를 잡을 수 있어요? (Yeogiseo taeksileul jabeul su isseoyo?)

Can I get a taxi here? 여기서 택시를 잡을 수 있어요? (Yeogiseo taeksileul jabeul su isseoyo?)

How much does a taxi to the hotel cost? 호텔까지 택시비 얼마에요? (Hotelkkaji taeksibi eolmaeyo?)

How much does a taxi to the hotel cost? 호텔까지 택시비 얼마에요? (Hotelkkaji taeksibi eolmaeyo?)

What platform is the train to Busan? 부산행 기차는 몇 번 승강장에 가나요? (Busanhaeng gichaneun myeot beon seunggangjange ganaeyo?)

What platform is the train to Busan? 부산행 기차는 몇 번 승강장에 가나요? (Busanhaeng gichaneun myeot beon seunggangjange ganaeyo?)

I need to change terminals. 터미널을 바꿔야 해요. (Teomineoreul bakkwoya haeyo.)

I need to change terminals. 터미널을 바꿔야 해요. (Teomineoreul bakkwoya haeyo.)

Where is the customs office? 세관 사무실은 어디에요? (Segwan samusileun eodieyo?)

Where is the customs office? 세관 사무실은 어디에요? (Segwan samusileun eodieyo?)

Can I use Wi-Fi here? 여기서 와이파이를 사용할 수 있어요? (Yeogiseo waipaireul sayonghal su isseoyo?)

Can I use Wi-Fi here? 여기서 와이파이를 사용할 수 있어요? (Yeogiseo waipaireul sayonghal su isseoyo?)

What time is the boarding for my flight? 제 비행기 탑승 시간이 언제에요? (Je bihaenggi tabseung sigani eonjeyo?)

What time is the boarding for my flight? 제 비행기 탑승 시간이 언제에요? (Je bihaenggi tabseung sigani eonjeyo?)

Is there a currency exchange nearby? 근처에 환전소가 있나요? (Geuncheoe hwanjeonso-ga issnayo?)

Is there a currency exchange nearby? 근처에 환전소가 있나요? (Geuncheoe hwanjeonso-ga issnayo?)

My flight is delayed. 제 비행기가 지연돼요. (Je bihaenggi-ga jiyeondwaeyo.)

My flight is delayed. 제 비행기가 지연돼요. (Je bihaenggi-ga jiyeondwaeyo.)

Do you have a map of the airport? 공항지도 있어요? (Gonghang jido isseoyo?)

Do you have a map of the airport? 공항지도 있어요? (Gonghang jido isseoyo?)

Where can I buy a SIM card for my phone? 핸드폰용 심카드 어디에서 사나요? (Haendeupon-yong simkadeu eodieeseo sanaeyo?)

Where can I buy a SIM card for my phone? 핸드폰용 심카드 어디에서 사나요? (Haendeupon-yong simkadeu eodieeseo sanaeyo?)

I lost my luggage. 제 수하물을 잃어버렸어요. (Je suhamureul ilheobeoryeosseoyo.)

I lost my luggage. 제 수하물을 잃어버렸어요. (Je suhamureul ilheobeoryeosseoyo.)

How far is the hotel from the airport? 호텔이 공항에서 얼마나 떨어져 있어요? (Hotel-i gonghangeseo eolmana tteoreojyeo isseoyo?)

How far is the hotel from the airport? 호텔이 공항에서 얼마나 떨어져 있어요? (Hotel-i gonghangeseo eolmana tteoreojyeo isseoyo?)

Is there a pharmacy in the airport? 공항에 약국이 있나요? (Gonghang-e yakguk-i issnayo?)

Is there a pharmacy in the airport? 공항에 약국이 있나요? (Gonghang-e yakguk-i issnayo?)

I need a taxi to the airport. 공항까지 택시를 부를게요. (Gonghangkkaji taeksireul bureulgeyo.)

I need a taxi to the airport. 공항까지 택시를 부를게요. (Gonghangkkaji taeksireul bureulgeyo.)

Can I have a receipt, please? 영수증 좀 받을 수 있을까요? (Yeongsujeung jom badeul su isseulkkayo?)

Can I have a receipt, please? 영수증 좀 받을 수 있을까요? (Yeongsujeung jom badeul su isseulkkayo?)

What gate is my flight departing from? 제 비행기는 몇 번 출발 게이트에서 나가나요? (Je bihaenggi-neun myeot beon chulbal geiteueseo nanagayo?)

What gate is my flight departing from? 제 비행기는 몇 번 출발 게이트에서 나가나요? (Je bihaenggi-neun myeot beon chulbal geiteueseo nanagayo?)

Where can I find a good restaurant here? 여기서 좋은 음식점 어디에요? (Yeogiseo joh-eun eumsigjeom eodieyo?)

Where can I find a good restaurant here? 여기서 좋은 음식점 어디에요? (Yeogiseo joh-eun eumsigjeom eodieyo?)

Can you recommend a local dish to try? 시키지 못할 지역 음식 하나 추천해 주실 수 있나요? (Sikji mothal jyeog eumsik hana chucheonhae jushil su issnayo?)

Can you recommend a local dish to try? 시키지 못할 지역 음식 하나 추천해 주실 수 있나요? (Sikji mothal jyeog eumsik hana chucheonhae jushil su issnayo?)

What time does the airport shuttle bus leave? 공항 셔틀 버스는 몇 시에 떠나나요? (Gonghang syeoteul beoseuneun myeot sie tteonanayo?)

What time does the airport shuttle bus leave? 공항 셔틀 버스는 몇 시에 떠나나요? (Gonghang syeoteul beoseuneun myeot sie tteonanayo?)

Where is the nearest ATM? 가장 가까운 ATM은 어디에요? (Gajang gakkawoon ATM-eun eodieyo?)

Where is the nearest ATM? 가장 가까운 ATM은 어디에요? (Gajang gakkawoon ATM-eun eodieyo?)

I need to pick up a rental car. 렌터카를 찾아가야 해요. (Renteokareul chajagaya haeyo.)

I need to pick up a rental car. 렌터카를 찾아가야 해요. (Renteokareul chajagaya haeyo.)

Is there a lost and found office? 분실물 보관소가 있나요? (Bunsilmul bogwanso-ga issnayo?)

Is there a lost and found office? 분실물 보관소가 있나요? (Bunsilmul bogwanso-ga issnayo?)

What is the duty-free limit for purchases? 면세품 구매 한도가 얼마에요? (Myeonsaepum guma handoga eolmaeyo?)

What is the duty-free limit for purchases? 면세품 구매 한도가 얼마에요? (Myeonsaepum guma handoga eolmaeyo?)

Can I bring this through security? 이걸 보안 검색을 통과할 수 있어요? (Igeol boan geomseogeul tonggwahal su isseoyo?)

Can I bring this through security? 이걸 보안 검색을 통과할 수 있어요? (Igeol boan geomseogeul tonggwahal su isseoyo?)

Is there a place to store my luggage temporarily? 잠시 동안 수하물을 보관할 수 있는 곳이 있나요? (Jamsi dongan suhamureul bogwanhal su issneun gosi issnayo?)

Is there a place to store my luggage temporarily? 잠시 동안 수하물을 보관할 수 있는 곳이 있나요? (Jamsi dongan suhamureul bogwanhal su issneun gosi issnayo?)

What is the boarding gate for international flights? 국제선 비행기 탑승문은 어디에요? (Gukjesun bihaenggi tabseungmuneun eodieyo?)

What is the boarding gate for international flights? 국제선 비행기 탑승문은 어디에요? (Gukjesun bihaenggi tabseungmuneun eodieyo?)

Can I smoke in the designated areas? 흡연 구역에서 흡연할 수 있나요? (Heubyeon gueogeseo heubyeonhal su issnayo?)

Can I smoke in the designated areas? 흡연 구역에서 흡연할 수 있나요? (Heubyeon gueogeseo heubyeonhal su issnayo?)

How much is the airport parking fee? 공항 주차 요금은 얼마에요? (Gonghang jucha yogumeun eolmaeyo?)

How much is the airport parking fee? 공항 주차 요금은 얼마에요? (Gonghang jucha yogumeun eolmaeyo?)

What gate do I go to for connecting flights? 환승편을 타려면 어떤 출발 게이트로 가야 하나요? (Hwanseungpyeon-eul talyeomyeon eotteon chulbal geiteuro gaya hanayo?)

What gate do I go to for connecting flights? 환승편을 타려면 어떤 출발 게이트로 가야 하나요? (Hwanseungpyeon-eul talyeomyeon eotteon chulbal geiteuro gaya hanayo?)

Is there a place to buy travel adapters? 여행용 어댑터를 살 수 있는 곳이 있나요? (Yeohaengyong eodeobeoreul sal su issneun gosi issnayo?)

Is there a place to buy travel adapters? 여행용 어댑터를 살 수 있는 곳이 있나요? (Yeohaengyong eodeobeoreul sal su issneun gosi issnayo?)

Can I use my credit card here? 여기서 신용카드를 사용할 수 있어요? (Yeogiseo sinyongkadeu-reul sayonghal su isseoyo?)

Can I use my credit card here? 여기서 신용카드를 사용할 수 있어요? (Yeogiseo sinyongkadeu-reul sayonghal su isseoyo?)

Where is the information desk? 안내데스크는 어디에요? (Annae desk-neun eodieyo?)

Where is the information desk? 안내데스크는 어디에요? (Annae desk-neun eodieyo?)

What time does the last shuttle bus leave? 마지막 셔틀 버스는 몇 시에 떠나나요? (Majimak syeoteul beoseuneun myeot sie tteonanayo?)

What time does the last shuttle bus leave? 마지막 셔틀 버스는 몇 시에 떠나나요? (Majimak syeoteul beoseuneun myeot sie tteonanayo?)

Can I buy a local SIM card at the airport? 공항에서 지역 SIM 카드를 구입할 수 있나요? (Gonghangeseo jyeok SIM kadeu-reul gubiphal su issnayo?)

Can I buy a local SIM card at the airport? 공항에서 지역 SIM 카드를 구입할 수 있나요? (Gonghangeseo jyeok SIM kadeu-reul gubiphal su issnayo?)

Are there any restrictions on carrying liquids? 액체를 가지고 들어가는 데 제한사항이 있나요? (Aekcherul gajigo deul-eoganeun de jehansahang-i issnayo?)

Are there any restrictions on carrying liquids? 액체를 가지고 들어가는 데 제한사항이 있나요? (Aekcherul gajigo deul-eoganeun de jehansahang-i issnayo?)

What is the exchange rate for US dollars? 미국 달러의 환율은 어떻게 돼요? (Miguk dallele hwan-yuleun eotteohge dwaeyo?)

What is the exchange rate for US dollars? 미국 달러의 환율은 어떻게 돼요? (Miguk dallele hwan-yuleun eotteohge dwaeyo?)

Can I get a cart for my luggage? 수하물을 실을 카트를 어디서 얻을 수 있어요? (Suhamul-eul sil-eul katuleul eodieseo-eodeul su isseoyo?)

Can I get a cart for my luggage? 수하물을 실을 카트를 어디서 얻을 수 있어요? (Suhamul-eul sil-eul katuleul eodieseo-eodeul su isseoyo?)

Where is the closest restroom? 가장 가까운 화장실은 어디에요? (Gajang gakkawoon hwajangsil-eun eodieyo?)

Where is the closest restroom? 가장 가까운 화장실은 어디에요? (Gajang gakkawoon hwajangsil-eun eodieyo?)

Do I need to go through security again for a connecting flight? 환승편을 위해 다시 보안 검색을 받아야 하나요? (Hwanseungpyeon-eul wihae dasi boan geomseogeul bad-aya hanayo?)

Do I need to go through security again for a connecting flight? 환승편을 위해 다시 보안 검색을 받아야 하나요? (Hwanseungpyeon-eul wihae dasi boan geomseogeul bad-aya hanayo?)

What time does the airport close? 공항이 몇 시에 문을 닫나요? (Gonghang-i myeot sie mun-eul datnayo?)

What time does the airport close? 공항이 몇 시에 문을 닫나요? (Gonghang-i myeot sie mun-eul datnayo?)

Can I bring food from outside into the airport? 외부에서 음식을 공항으로 가져올 수 있나요?

(Oebu-eseo eumsig-eul gonghang-euro gajyeool su issnayo?)

Can I bring food from outside into the airport? 외부에서 음식을 공항으로 가져올 수 있나요? (Oebu-eseo eumsig-eul gonghang-euro gajyeool su issnayo?)

Is there a place to print my boarding pass? 탑승권을 출력할 수 있는 곳이 있나요? (Tabseung-gwon-eul chulchughal su issneun gosi issnayo?)

Is there a place to print my boarding pass? 탑승권을 출력할 수 있는 곳이 있나요? (Tabseung-gwon-eul chulchughal su issneun gosi issnayo?)

How long is the layover between flights? 비행기 간의 환승 시간은 얼마나 걸려요? (Bihaenggi ganui hwanseung siganeun eolmana geollyeoyo?)

How long is the layover between flights? 비행기 간의 환승 시간은 얼마나 걸려요? (Bihaenggi ganui hwanseung siganeun eolmana geollyeoyo?)

Can I use my mobile phone during the flight? 비행 중에 핸드폰을 사용할 수 있나요? (Bihaeng jung-e haendeupon-eul sayonghal su issnayo?)

Can I use my mobile phone during the flight? 비행 중에 핸드폰을 사용할 수 있나요? (Bihaeng jung-e haendeupon-eul sayonghal su issnayo?)

Is there a place to store my carry-on luggage? 소형 수하물을 보관할 수 있는 곳이 있나요? (Sohyeong suhamul-eul bogwanhal su issneun gosi issnayo?)

Is there a place to store my carry-on luggage? 소형 수하물을 보관할 수 있는 곳이 있나요? (Sohyeong suhamul-eul bogwanhal su issneun gosi issnayo?)

Are there any duty-free shops after security? 보안 검색 후 면세점이 있나요? (Boan geomseog hu myeonsaejeom-i issnayo?)

Are there any duty-free shops after security? 보안 검색 후 면세점이 있나요? (Boan geomseog hu myeonsaejeom-i issnayo?)

Can I upgrade my seat to business class? 내 좌석을 비즈니스 클래스로 업그레이드할 수 있나요? (Nae jwaseog-eul bizeuniseu keullaeseu-lo eobgeuleideu hal su issnayo?)

Can I upgrade my seat to business class? 내 좌석을 비즈니스 클래스로 업그레이드할 수 있나요? (Nae jwaseog-eul bizeuniseu keullaeseu-lo eobgeuleideu hal su issnayo?)

What terminal does the airport express train depart from? 공항 익스프레스 기차는 어떤 터미널에서 출발하나요? (Gonghang igseupeureseu gichaneun eotteon teomineol-eseo chulbalhanayo?)

What terminal does the airport express train depart from? 공항 익스프레스 기차는 어떤 터미널에서

출발하나요? (Gonghang igseupeureseu gichaneun eotteon teomineol-eseo chulbalhanayo?)

Can I bring my pet on the flight? 비행기에 애완동물을 데리고 갈 수 있나요? (Bihaenggi-e aewandongmul-eul deligo gal su issnayo?)

Can I bring my pet on the flight? 비행기에 애완동물을 데리고 갈 수 있나요? (Bihaenggi-e aewandongmul-eul deligo gal su issnayo?)

How much is the excess baggage fee? 초과 수하물 수수료는 얼마에요? (Chogwa suhamul susuloneun eolmaeyo?)

How much is the excess baggage fee? 초과 수하물 수수료는 얼마에요? (Chogwa suhamul susuloneun eolmaeyo?)

Is there a place to get a massage in the airport? 공항에 마사지를 받을 수 있는 곳이 있나요? (Gonghang-e masajileul badeul su issneun gosi issnayo?)

Is there a place to get a massage in the airport? 공항에 마사지를 받을 수 있는 곳이 있나요? (Gonghang-e masajileul badeul su issneun gosi issnayo?)

Can I check in online for my flight? 제 비행기를 온라인으로 체크인할 수 있나요? (Je bihaenggi-reul onlain-euro chekeu-inhal su issnayo?)

Can I check in online for my flight? 제 비행기를 온라인으로 체크인할 수 있나요? (Je bihaenggi-reul onlain-euro chekeu-inhal su issnayo?)

Are there any vegetarian options at the airport restaurants? 공항 식당에서 채식주의자 옵션이 있나요? (Gonghang sikdang-eseo chaesikjuuija opseu-i issnayo?)

Are there any vegetarian options at the airport restaurants? 공항 식당에서 채식주의자 옵션이 있나요? (Gonghang sikdang-eseo chaesikjuuija opseu-i issnayo?)

Is there a medical center in the airport? 공항에 의료 센터가 있나요? (Gonghang-e uilyo sente-ga issnayo?)

Is there a medical center in the airport? 공항에 의료 센터가 있나요? (Gonghang-e uilyo sente-ga issnayo?)

Can I buy a ticket for the airport shuttle bus on board? 공항 셔틀 버스 표는 차 안에서 살 수 있나요? (Gonghang syeoteul beoseu pyo-neun cha an-eseo sal su issnayo?)

Can I buy a ticket for the airport shuttle bus on board? 공항 셔틀 버스 표는 차 안에서 살 수 있나요? (Gonghang syeoteul beoseu pyo-neun cha an-eseo sal su issnayo?)

What is the limit for duty-free alcohol purchases? 면세주류 구매 한도가 얼마에요? (Myeonsaejulyu guma handoga eolmaeyo?)

What is the limit for duty-free alcohol purchases? 면세주류 구매 한도가 얼마에요? (Myeonsaejulyu guma handoga eolmaeyo?)

Leisure and Entertainment:

I bought tickets for the concert. - 나는 콘서트를 위한 티켓을 샀어요. (Naneun konseoteu-reul wihan tiket-eul sasseoyo.)

I bought tickets for the concert. - 나는 콘서트를 위한 티켓을 샀어요. (Naneun konseoteu-reul wihan tiket-eul sasseoyo.)

Are you coming to the theater tonight? - 오늘 밤 극장에 오시나요? (Oneul bam geukjang-e osinayo?)

Are you coming to the theater tonight? - 오늘 밤 극장에 오시나요? (Oneul bam geukjang-e osinayo?)

She loves going to live performances. - 그녀는 라이브 공연을 좋아해요. (Geunyeoneun laibeu gongyeon-eul johahaeyo.)

She loves going to live performances. - 그녀는 라이브 공연을 좋아해요. (Geunyeoneun laibeu gongyeon-eul johahaeyo.)

We have reserved seats for the play. - 우리는 연극을 위한 좌석을 예약했어요. (Ulineun yeongeuk-eul wihan jwaseog-eul yeyaghayeosseoyo.)

We have reserved seats for the play. - 우리는 연극을 위한 좌석을 예약했어요. (Ulineun yeongeuk-eul wihan jwaseog-eul yeyaghayeosseoyo.)

Let's enjoy the festival together. - 함께 축제를 즐겨봐요. (Hamkke chukjeleul jeulgyeobwayo.)

Let's enjoy the festival together. - 함께 축제를 즐겨봐요. (Hamkke chukjeleul jeulgyeobwayo.)

The sports match is starting soon. - 스포츠 경기가 곧 시작돼요. (Seupocheu gyeong-giga got sijakdwaeyo.)

The sports match is starting soon. - 스포츠 경기가 곧 시작돼요. (Seupocheu gyeong-giga got sijakdwaeyo.)

He is a fan of classical music. - 그는 고전 음악 팬이에요. (Geuneun gojeon eumak paen-ieyo.)

He is a fan of classical music. - 그는 고전 음악 팬이에요. (Geuneun gojeon eumak paen-ieyo.)

I want to watch a movie this weekend. - 이번 주말에 영화를 보고 싶어요. (Ibeon jumal-e yeonghwa-reul bogo sip-eoyo.)

I want to watch a movie this weekend. - 이번 주말에 영화를 보고 싶어요. (Ibeon jumal-e yeonghwa-reul bogo sip-eoyo.)

Let's go out for dinner tomorrow. - 내일 저녁에 식사하러 가요. (Naeil jeonyeok-e sigsahaleo gayo.)

Let's go out for dinner tomorrow. - 내일 저녁에 식사하러 가요. (Naeil jeonyeok-e sigsahaleo gayo.)

What about a picnic in the park? - 공원에서 소풍 어때요? (Gongwon-eseo sopung eottaeyo?)

What about a picnic in the park? - 공원에서 소풍 어때요? (Gongwon-eseo sopung eottaeyo?)

Shall we go hiking this Saturday? - 이번 주 토요일에 등산가요? (Ibeon ju toyoil-e deungsangaeyo?)

Shall we go hiking this Saturday? - 이번 주 토요일에 등산가요? (Ibeon ju toyoil-e deungsangaeyo?)

I'm planning a game night at my place. - 내 집에서 게임 밤을 계획 중이에요. (Nae jib-eseo geim bam-eul gyehoek jung-ieyo.)

I'm planning a game night at my place. - 내 집에서 게임 밤을 계획 중이에요. (Nae jib-eseo geim bam-eul gyehoek jung-ieyo.)

How about trying a new restaurant? - 새로운 음식점을 시도해볼까요? (Saeroun eumsigjeom-eul sidoaebolkkaayo?)

How about trying a new restaurant? - 새로운 음식점을 시도해볼까요? (Saeroun eumsigjeom-eul sidoaebolkkaayo?)

We can meet at the coffee shop. - 커피숍에서 만날 수 있어요. (Keopis-sob-eso mannal su iss-eoyo.)

We can meet at the coffee shop. - 커피숍에서 만날 수 있어요. (Keopis-sob-eso mannal su iss-eoyo.)

Let's have a barbecue this Sunday. - 이번 주 일요일에 바베큐 해요. (Ibeon ju il-yoil-e babekyu haeyo.)

Let's have a barbecue this Sunday. - 이번 주 일요일에 바베큐 해요. (Ibeon ju il-yoil-e babekyu haeyo.)

Do you want to join a dance class? - 댄스 수업에 참여하고 싶어요. (Daenseu sueob-e chamyeo hago sip-eoyo.)

Do you want to join a dance class? - 댄스 수업에 참여하고 싶어요. (Daenseu sueob-e chamyeo hago sip-eoyo.)

We should visit the art exhibition. - 우리는 미술 전시회를 방문해야 해요. (Ulineun misul jeonsihoeleul bangmunhaeya haeyo.)

We should visit the art exhibition. - 우리는 미술 전시회를 방문해야 해요. (Ulineun misul jeonsihoeleul bangmunhaeya haeyo.)

How about a beach day next week? - 다음 주에 해변에 가볼까요? (Daeum ju-e haebon-e gabolkkaayo?)

How about a beach day next week? - 다음 주에 해변에 가볼까요? (Daeum ju-e haebon-e gabolkkaayo?)

I enjoy reading novels in my free time. - 나는 여가 시간에 소설 읽는 것을 즐겨요. (Naneun yeoga sigan-e sosol ilg-eun geos-eul jeulg-yeoyo.)

I enjoy reading novels in my free time. - 나는 여가 시간에 소설 읽는 것을 즐겨요. (Naneun yeoga sigan-e sosol ilg-eun geos-eul jeulg-yeoyo.)

What kind of music do you like? - 어떤 종류의 음악을 좋아해요? (Eotteon jonglyu-e eum-ag-eul johahaeyo?)

What kind of music do you like? - 어떤 종류의 음악을 좋아해요? (Eotteon jonglyu-e eum-ag-eul johahaeyo?)

Painting is my favorite hobby. - 그림 그리기가 제 가장 좋아하는 취미에요. (Geulim geuligi-ga je gajang johahaneun chwimi-eoyo.)

Painting is my favorite hobby. - 그림 그리기가 제 가장 좋아하는 취미에요. (Geulim geuligi-ga je gajang johahaneun chwimi-eoyo.)

Let's play board games this evening. - 오늘 저녁에 보드 게임을 하자. (Oneul jeonyeok-e bodeu geim-eul haja.)

Let's play board games this evening. - 오늘 저녁에 보드 게임을 하자. (Oneul jeonyeok-e bodeu geim-eul haja.)

I love cooking new recipes. - 나는 새로운 요리를 만드는 것을 좋아해요. (Naneun saeloun yolileul mandeuneun geos-eul johahaeyo.)

I love cooking new recipes. - 나는 새로운 요리를 만드는 것을 좋아해요. (Naneun saeloun yolileul mandeuneun geos-eul johahaeyo.)

Photography is a fascinating hobby. - 사진 찍기는 매력적인 취미에요. (Sajin jjig-gineun maelyeogjeog-in chwimi-eoyo.)

Photography is a fascinating hobby. - 사진 찍기는 매력적인 취미에요. (Sajin jjig-gineun maelyeogjeog-in chwimi-eoyo.)

I'm a big fan of science fiction movies. - 나는 공상 과학 영화의 열렬한 팬이에요. (Naneun gongsang gwahag yeonghwa-ui yeollyeolhan paen-ieyo.)

I'm a big fan of science fiction movies. - 나는 공상 과학 영화의 열렬한 팬이에요. (Naneun gongsang gwahag yeonghwa-ui yeollyeolhan paen-ieyo.)

Playing musical instruments is relaxing. - 악기 연주는 편안한 것 같아요. (Aggi yeonju-neun pyeon-anhan geos gat-aoyo.)

Playing musical instruments is relaxing. - 악기 연주는 편안한 것 같아요. (Aggi yeonju-neun pyeon-anhan geos gat-aoyo.)

Let's go cycling in the countryside. - 시골에서 자전거 타러 가요. (Sigol-eseo jajeongeo taleo gayo.)

Let's go cycling in the countryside. - 시골에서 자전거 타러 가요. (Sigol-eseo jajeongeo taleo gayo.)

I collect vintage postcards. - 나는 빈티지 엽서를 수집해요. (Naneun bintiji yeobseoleul sujibhaeyo.)

I collect vintage postcards. - 나는 빈티지 엽서를 수집해요. (Naneun bintiji yeobseoleul sujibhaeyo.)

Gardening is therapeutic for me. - 정원 일하기는 나에게 치유의 과정이에요. (Jeongwon ilhagineun naege chiyuui gwajeong-ieyo.)

Gardening is therapeutic for me. - 정원 일하기는 나에게 치유의 과정이에요. (Jeongwon ilhagineun naege chiyuui gwajeong-ieyo.)

I'm passionate about learning new languages. - 나는 새로운 언어를 배우는 데 열정적이에요. (Naneun saeloun eon-eoleul baeuneun de yeoljeongjeog-ieyo.)

I'm passionate about learning new languages. - 나는 새로운 언어를 배우는 데 열정적이에요. (Naneun saeloun eon-eoleul baeuneun de yeoljeongjeog-ieyo.)

Let's go fishing this weekend. - 이번 주말에 낚시하러 가요. (Ibeon jumal-e najsihaleo gayo.)

Let's go fishing this weekend. - 이번 주말에 낚시하러 가요. (Ibeon jumal-e najsihaleo gayo.)

Traveling is a great way to explore. - 여행은 탐험하는 좋은 방법이에요. (Yeohaeng-eun tamheomhaneun joh-eun bangbeob-ieyo.)

Traveling is a great way to explore. - 여행은 탐험하는 좋은 방법이에요. (Yeohaeng-eun tamheomhaneun joh-eun bangbeob-ieyo.)

I like attending art workshops. - 나는 예술 워크샵에 참여하는 것을 좋아해요. (Naneun yesul wokeusyab-e chamyeo haneun geos-eul johahaeyo.)

I like attending art workshops. - 나는 예술 워크샵에 참여하는 것을 좋아해요. (Naneun yesul wokeusyab-e chamyeo haneun geos-eul johahaeyo.)

Let's go to a comedy show. - 코미디 쇼에 가볼까요? (Komidi syo-e gabolkkaayo?)

Let's go to a comedy show. - 코미디 쇼에 가볼까요? (Komidi syo-e gabolkkaayo?)

Chess is a strategic and fun game. - 체스는 전략적이고 재미있는 게임이에요. (Cheseu-neun jeollaejeog-igo jaemiissneun geim-ieyo.)

Chess is a strategic and fun game. - 체스는 전략적이고 재미있는 게임이에요. (Cheseu-neun jeollaejeog-igo jaemiissneun geim-ieyo.)

Technology and Connectivity:

May I have the Wi-Fi password, please? - 와이파이 비밀번호 주세요 (waipa-i bimilbeonho juseyo).

May I have the Wi-Fi password, please? - 와이파이 비밀번호 주세요 (waipa-i bimilbeonho juseyo).

What's the password for the Wi-Fi network? - 와이파이 네트워크 비밀번호가 뭐에요? (waipa-i neteuwokeu bimilbeonhoga mwoeyo?).

What's the password for the Wi-Fi network? - 와이파이 네트워크 비밀번호가 뭐에요? (waipa-i neteuwokeu bimilbeonhoga mwoeyo?).

My computer is not working properly. - 제 컴퓨터가 제대로 작동하지 않아요 (je keompyuteoga jedaero jakdonghaji anayo).

My computer is not working properly. - 제 컴퓨터가 제대로 작동하지 않아요 (je keompyuteoga jedaero jakdonghaji anayo).

I'm experiencing issues with my smartphone. - 제 스마트폰에 문제가 있어요 (je seumateupon-e munjega isseoyo).

I'm experiencing issues with my smartphone. - 제 스마트폰에 문제가 있어요 (je seumateupon-e munjega isseoyo).

Can I charge my phone here? - 여기서 핸드폰 충전할 수 있어요? (yeogiseo haendeupon chungjeonhal su isseoyo?).

Can I charge my phone here? - 여기서 핸드폰 충전할 수 있어요? (yeogiseo haendeupon chungjeonhal su isseoyo?).

I need to buy a new charger for my tablet. - 제 태블릿을 위한 새로운 충전기를 사야 해요 (je taebelriseul wihan saeroun chungjeongireul saya haeyo).

I need to buy a new charger for my tablet. - 제 태블릿을 위한 새로운 충전기를 사야 해요 (je taebelriseul wihan saeroun chungjeongireul saya haeyo).

I love the convenience of online shopping. - 온라인 쇼핑의 편리함을 정말 좋아해요 (onlain shopping-ui pyeonrihameul jeongmal johahaeyo).

I love the convenience of online shopping. - 온라인 쇼핑의 편리함을 정말 좋아해요 (onlain shopping-ui pyeonrihameul jeongmal johahaeyo).

Technology has made communication so much easier. - 기술 덕분에 소통이 훨씬 쉬워졌어요 (gisul deokbune sotong-i hwolssin swoweojyeosseoyo).

Technology has made communication so much easier. - 기술 덕분에 소통이 훨씬 쉬워졌어요

(gisul deokbune sotong-i hwolssin swoweojyeosseoyo).

Turn off the lights, please. - 등을 끄세요 (deung-eul kkeuseyo).

Turn off the lights, please. - 등을 끄세요 (deung-eul kkeuseyo).

Set the thermostat to 23 degrees Celsius. - 온도를 23도로 설정해 주세요 (ondo-reul 23-doro seoljeonghae juseyo).

Set the thermostat to 23 degrees Celsius. - 온도를 23도로 설정해 주세요 (ondo-reul 23-doro seoljeonghae juseyo).

My internet connection is very slow. - 인터넷 연결이 매우 느려요 (inteoneseut yeon-gyeol-i ma-u neulyeo-yo).

My internet connection is very slow. - 인터넷 연결이 매우 느려요 (inteoneseut yeon-gyeol-i ma-u neulyeo-yo).

I can't seem to connect to the Bluetooth device. - 블루투스 장치에 연결이 안 돼요 (beullutuseu jangchi-e yeon-gyeol-i an dwae-yo).

I can't seem to connect to the Bluetooth device. - 블루투스 장치에 연결이 안 돼요 (beullutuseu jangchi-e yeon-gyeol-i an dwae-yo).

Can you recommend a good antivirus software? - 좋은 백신 소프트웨어 추천해 주실 수 있나요?

(joh-eun baegsin sopeutuweeo chucheonhae jusil su issnayo?)

Can you recommend a good antivirus software? - 좋은 백신 소프트웨어 추천해 주실 수 있나요? (joh-eun baegsin sopeutuweeo chucheonhae jusil su issnayo?)

What's the best brand for laptops in Korea? - 한국에서 노트북으로는 어떤 브랜드가 최고에요? (hanguk-eseo noteubug-euloneun eod-eon beulaendeu-ga choegoe-yo?)

What's the best brand for laptops in Korea? - 한국에서 노트북으로는 어떤 브랜드가 최고에요? (hanguk-eseo noteubug-euloneun eod-eon beulaendeu-ga choegoe-yo?)

There's a software update available. - 소프트웨어 업데이트가 가능해요 (sopeutuweeo eopdeiteu-ga ganeunghaeyo).

There's a software update available. - 소프트웨어 업데이트가 가능해요 (sopeutuweeo eopdeiteu-ga ganeunghaeyo).

Should I install the latest system update? - 최신 시스템 업데이트를 설치해야 할까요? (choesin siseutem eopdeiteu-leul seolchihaeya halkka-yo?)

Should I install the latest system update? - 최신 시스템 업데이트를 설치해야 할까요? (choesin siseutem eopdeiteu-leul seolchihaeya halkka-yo?)

I posted a new photo on Instagram. - 인스타그램에 새로운 사진을 올렸어요 (inseutageulaem-e saeroun sajin-eul ollyeosseoyo).

I posted a new photo on Instagram. - 인스타그램에 새로운 사진을 올렸어요 (inseutageulaem-e saeroun sajin-eul ollyeosseoyo).

Let's chat on KakaoTalk later. - 나중에 카카오톡으로 얘기하자 (najung-e kakaotog-euro yaegihaja).

Let's chat on KakaoTalk later. - 나중에 카카오톡으로 얘기하자 (najung-e kakaotog-euro yaegihaja).

Can we schedule a Zoom meeting for tomorrow? - 내일 줌 미팅을 예약할 수 있을까요? (naeil jum miteung-eul yeyakhal su iss-eulkka-yo?)

Can we schedule a Zoom meeting for tomorrow? - 내일 줌 미팅을 예약할 수 있을까요? (naeil jum miteung-eul yeyakhal su iss-eulkka-yo?)

I'll send you the Microsoft Teams link. - 마이크로소프트 팀즈 링크를 보내 드릴게요 (maikeuloseupoteu timjeu lingkeu-reul bonaedeulilgeyo).

I'll send you the Microsoft Teams link. - 마이크로소프트 팀즈 링크를 보내 드릴게요 (maikeuloseupoteu timjeu lingkeu-reul bonaedeulilgeyo).

Is there free Wi-Fi in this cafe? - 이 카페에 무료 와이파이가 있나요? (i kape-e mulo waipa-i-ga issnayo?)

Is there free Wi-Fi in this cafe? - 이 카페에 무료 와이파이가 있나요? (i kape-e mulo waipa-i-ga issnayo?)

My phone battery is running low. - 핸드폰 배터리가 거의 다 떨어졌어요 (haendeupon baeteoli-ga geoui da tteo-eojyeosseoyo).

My phone battery is running low. - 핸드폰 배터리가 거의 다 떨어졌어요 (haendeupon baeteoli-ga geoui da tteo-eojyeosseoyo).

The app keeps crashing on my tablet. - 어플이 제 태블릿에서 계속 다운돼요 (eopeuli je taebelriseo gyesok daundwaeyo).

The app keeps crashing on my tablet. - 어플이 제 태블릿에서 계속 다운돼요 (eopeuli je taebelriseo gyesok daundwaeyo).

Can you show me how to use this new gadget? - 이 신제품 사용법 좀 알려 주세요 (i shinjepum sayongbeop jom allyeo juseyo).

Can you show me how to use this new gadget? - 이 신제품 사용법 좀 알려 주세요 (i shinjepum sayongbeop jom allyeo juseyo).

I accidentally deleted an important file. - 실수로 중요한 파일을 삭제했어요 (sil-sulo jung-yohan paileul saelchyeo-haes-eoyo).

I accidentally deleted an important file. - 실수로 중요한 파일을 삭제했어요 (sil-sulo jung-yohan paileul saelchyeo-haes-eoyo).

I need to update my antivirus software. - 제 백신 소프트웨어를 업데이트해야 해요 (je baegsin sopeutuweeo-leul eopdeiteuhaeya haeyo).

I need to update my antivirus software. - 제 백신 소프트웨어를 업데이트해야 해요 (je baegsin sopeutuweeo-leul eopdeiteuhaeya haeyo).

Can you recommend a reliable tech support service? - 믿을 수 있는 기술 지원 서비스를 추천해 주실 수 있나요? (mid-eul su issneun gisul jiweon seobiseu-leul chucheonhae jusil su issnayo?)

Can you recommend a reliable tech support service? - 믿을 수 있는 기술 지원 서비스를 추천해 주실 수 있나요? (mid-eul su issneun gisul jiweon seobiseu-leul chucheonhae jusil su issnayo?)

I accidentally clicked on a phishing link. - 실수로 피싱 링크를 클릭했어요 (sil-sulo pising lingkeu-reul keullighaess-eoyo).

I accidentally clicked on a phishing link. - 실수로 피싱 링크를 클릭했어요 (sil-sulo pising lingkeu-reul keullighaess-eoyo).

The printer is not responding. - 프린터가 응답하지 않아요 (peurinteo-ga eungdap-haji anayo).

The printer is not responding. - 프린터가 응답하지 않아요 (peurinteo-ga eungdap-haji anayo).

How do I update the software on my smart TV? - 스마트 TV의 소프트웨어를 어떻게 업데이트하나요? (seumateu TV-ui sopeutuweeo-leul eotteohge eopdeiteu-hanayo?)

How do I update the software on my smart TV? - 스마트 TV의 소프트웨어를 어떻게 업데이트하나요? (seumateu TV-ui sopeutuweeo-leul eotteohge eopdeiteu-hanayo?)

Can I use Google Maps for navigation in Korea? - 한국에서 구글 맵을 길 안내에 사용할 수 있어요? (hanguk-eseo gugeul maeb-eul gil annae-e sayonghal su isseoyo?)

Can I use Google Maps for navigation in Korea? - 한국에서 구글 맵을 길 안내에 사용할 수 있어요? (hanguk-eseo gugeul maeb-eul gil annae-e sayonghal su isseoyo?)

My laptop is not connecting to the office VPN. - 제 노트북이 회사 VPN에 연결되지 않아요 (je noteubug-i hoesa VPN-e yeon-gyeol-doeji anayo).

My laptop is not connecting to the office VPN. - 제 노트북이 회사 VPN에 연결되지 않아요 (je noteubug-i hoesa VPN-e yeon-gyeol-doeji anayo).

What's the latest version of the operating system? - 최신 운영 체제의 버전이 뭐에요? (choesin unyeong cheje-ui beojeon-i mwoeyo?)

What's the latest version of the operating system? - 최신 운영 체제의 버전이 뭐에요? (choesin unyeong cheje-ui beojeon-i mwoeyo?)

How can I recover deleted files from my computer? - 컴퓨터에서 삭제된 파일을 어떻게 복구하나요? (keompyuteo-eseo saelchyeodwen paileul eotteohge bogguhanaeyo?)

How can I recover deleted files from my computer? - 컴퓨터에서 삭제된 파일을 어떻게 복구하나요? (keompyuteo-eseo saelchyeodwen paileul eotteohge bogguhanaeyo?)

I forgot my Apple ID password. - 애플 ID 비밀번호를 잊어버렸어요 (aepeul ID bimilbeonho-reul ijeobeoryeosseoyo).

I forgot my Apple ID password. - 애플 ID 비밀번호를 잊어버렸어요 (aepeul ID bimilbeonho-reul ijeobeoryeosseoyo).

Can you help me set up a password for my new phone? - 새 핸드폰에 비밀번호 설정하는 데 도와주실 수 있나요? (sae haendeupon-e bimilbeonho seoljeonghaneun de do-wajusil su issnayo?)

Can you help me set up a password for my new phone? - 새 핸드폰에 비밀번호 설정하는 데 도와주실 수 있나요? (sae haendeupon-e bimilbeonho seoljeonghaneun de do-wajusil su issnayo?)

My camera app is not working. - 카메라 어플이 작동하지 않아요 (kamera eopeuli jakdonghaji anayo).

My camera app is not working. - 카메라 어플이 작동하지 않아요 (kamera eopeuli jakdonghaji anayo).

I accidentally spilled water on my laptop. - 실수로 노트북에 물을 흘렸어요 (sil-sulo noteubug-e mul-eul heulleosseoyo).

I accidentally spilled water on my laptop. - 실수로 노트북에 물을 흘렸어요 (sil-sulo noteubug-e mul-eul heulleosseoyo).

Can you recommend a good podcast app? - 좋은 팟캐스트 어플 추천해 주실 수 있나요? (joh-eun patkaeseuteu eopeul chucheonhae jusil su issnayo?)

Can you recommend a good podcast app? - 좋은 팟캐스트 어플 추천해 주실 수 있나요? (joh-eun patkaeseuteu eopeul chucheonhae jusil su issnayo?)

How do I transfer photos from my phone to my computer? - 핸드폰에서 사진을 컴퓨터로 어떻게

옮기나요? (haendeupon-eseo sajin-eul keompyuteulo eotteohge olmyeonaeyo?)

How do I transfer photos from my phone to my computer? - 핸드폰에서 사진을 컴퓨터로 어떻게 옮기나요? (haendeupon-eseo sajin-eul keompyuteulo eotteohge olmyeonaeyo?)

I'm getting too many spam emails. - 스팸 메일이 너무 많이 와요 (seupaem meil-i neomu mani wayo).

I'm getting too many spam emails. - 스팸 메일이 너무 많이 와요 (seupaem meil-i neomu mani wayo).

Can you recommend a good gaming laptop? - 좋은 게이밍 노트북 추천해 주실 수 있나요? (joh-eun geiming noteubug chucheonhae jusil su issnayo?)

Can you recommend a good gaming laptop? - 좋은 게이밍 노트북 추천해 주실 수 있나요? (joh-eun geiming noteubug chucheonhae jusil su issnayo?)

My phone is not connecting to the mobile network. - 제 핸드폰이 이동 통신망에 연결되지 않아요 (je haendeupon-i idong tongshinmang-e yeon-gyeol-doeji anayo).

My phone is not connecting to the mobile network. - 제 핸드폰이 이동 통신망에 연결되지 않아요 (je haendeupon-i idong tongshinmang-e yeon-gyeol-doeji anayo).

What's the best way to back up my data? - 데이터를 백업하는 가장 좋은 방법은 뭐에요? (deiteo-leul baeg-eobhaneun gajang joh-eun bangbeob-eun mwoeyo?)

What's the best way to back up my data? - 데이터를 백업하는 가장 좋은 방법은 뭐에요? (deiteo-leul baeg-eobhaneun gajang joh-eun bangbeob-eun mwoeyo?)

How do I enable two-factor authentication on my account? - 내 계정에 이중 인증을 어떻게 활성화하나요? (nae gyejeon-e ijung injeung-eul eotteohge hwal-yeonhwahanaeyo?)

How do I enable two-factor authentication on my account? - 내 계정에 이중 인증을 어떻게 활성화하나요? (nae gyejeon-e ijung injeung-eul eotteohge hwal-yeonhwahanaeyo?)

My smartwatch is not syncing with my phone. - 제 스마트워치가 핸드폰과 동기화되지 않아요 (je seumateuwochi-ga haendeupongwa donggyihwadoeji anayo).

My smartwatch is not syncing with my phone. - 제 스마트워치가 핸드폰과 동기화되지 않아요 (je seumateuwochi-ga haendeupongwa donggyihwadoeji anayo).

Can you help me set up a VPN on my computer? - 컴퓨터에 VPN 설정하는 데 도와주실 수 있나요?

(keompyuteo-e VPN seoljeonghaneun de do-wajusil su issnayo?)

Can you help me set up a VPN on my computer? - 컴퓨터에 VPN 설정하는 데 도와주실 수 있나요? (keompyuteo-e VPN seoljeonghaneun de do-wajusil su issnayo?)

I accidentally deleted a text message. - 실수로 텍스트 메시지를 삭제했어요 (sil-sulo tekeusteuteu mesiji-leul saelchyeo-haes-eoyo).

I accidentally deleted a text message. - 실수로 텍스트 메시지를 삭제했어요 (sil-sulo tekeusteuteu mesiji-leul saelchyeo-haes-eoyo).

How do I stop automatic updates on my phone? - 핸드폰에서 자동 업데이트를 어떻게 멈출 수 있나요? (haendeupon-eseo jadong eopdeiteu-leul eotteohge meomchul su issnayo?)

How do I stop automatic updates on my phone? - 핸드폰에서 자동 업데이트를 어떻게 멈출 수 있나요? (haendeupon-eseo jadong eopdeiteu-leul eotteohge meomchul su issnayo?)

My laptop is not recognizing the external hard drive. - 제 노트북이 외장 하드 드라이브를 인식하지 않아요 (je noteubug-i oejang hadeu deuraibeu-leul insig-haji anayo).

My laptop is not recognizing the external hard drive. - 제 노트북이 외장 하드 드라이브를 인식하지

않아요 (je noteubug-i oejang hadeu deuraibeu-leul
insig-haji anayo).

Business and Professional Phrases:

Hello, it's nice to meet you. - 안녕하세요,
만나서 반갑습니다.

Hello, it's nice to meet you. - 안녕하세요,
만나서 반갑습니다.

Thank you for the opportunity. - 기회를 주셔서
감사합니다.

Thank you for the opportunity. - 기회를 주셔서
감사합니다.

Can we schedule a meeting? - 회의 일정을 잡을
수 있을까요?

Can we schedule a meeting? - 회의 일정을 잡을
수 있을까요?

I would like to discuss a potential collaboration. -
잠재적인 협업에 대해 이야기하고
싶습니다.

I would like to discuss a potential collaboration. -
잠재적인 협업에 대해 이야기하고
싶습니다.

Let's exchange business cards. - 명함을
교환하도록 하겠습니다.

Let's exchange business cards. - 명함을 교환하도록 하겠습니다.

What is your profession? - 당신은 어떤 직업을 가지고 계신가요?

What is your profession? - 당신은 어떤 직업을 가지고 계신가요?

I work in marketing. - 나는 마케팅 부문에서 일합니다.

I work in marketing. - 나는 마케팅 부문에서 일합니다.

Do you attend networking events often? - 자주 네트워킹 행사에 참석하시나요?

Do you attend networking events often? - 자주 네트워킹 행사에 참석하시나요?

Networking is crucial for career growth. - 네트워킹은 경력 성장에 중요합니다.

Networking is crucial for career growth. - 네트워킹은 경력 성장에 중요합니다.

Can I connect with you on LinkedIn? - LinkedIn에서 연결할 수 있을까요?

Can I connect with you on LinkedIn? - LinkedIn에서 연결할 수 있을까요?

I am interested in expanding my professional network. - 나는 전문 네트워크를 확장하는 것에 관심이 있습니다.

I am interested in expanding my professional network. - 나는 전문 네트워크를 확장하는 것에 관심이 있습니다.

Let's grab a coffee and discuss further. - 커피를 마시러 가서 더 자세히 얘기해봐요.

Let's grab a coffee and discuss further. - 커피를 마시러 가서 더 자세히 얘기해봐요.

I have an upcoming job interview. - 다가오는 취업 면접이 있습니다.

I have an upcoming job interview. - 다가오는 취업 면접이 있습니다.

Do you have any tips for a successful interview? - 성공적인 면접을 위한 조언이 있나요?

Do you have any tips for a successful interview? - 성공적인 면접을 위한 조언이 있나요?

Preparation is key for a job interview. - 면접 준비가 핵심입니다.

Preparation is key for a job interview. - 면접 준비가 핵심입니다.

Good luck with your interview! - 면접 잘 보세요!

Good luck with your interview! - 면접 잘 보세요!

The interview went well. - 면접이 잘 진행되었습니다.

The interview went well. - 면접이 잘 진행되었습니다.

I got the job! - 일자리를 얻었습니다!

I got the job! - 일자리를 얻었습니다!

I will be starting my new job next week. - 다음 주에 새로운 직장을 시작하게 됩니다.

I will be starting my new job next week. - 다음 주에 새로운 직장을 시작하게 됩니다.

What is your role in the company? - 회사에서 어떤 역할을 맡고 계세요?

What is your role in the company? - 회사에서 어떤 역할을 맡고 계세요?

I am responsible for project management. - 나는 프로젝트 관리를 담당하고 있습니다.

I am responsible for project management. - 나는 프로젝트 관리를 담당하고 있습니다.

Can we have a team meeting tomorrow? - 내일 팀 회의를 갖을 수 있을까요?

Can we have a team meeting tomorrow? - 내일 팀 회의를 갖을 수 있을까요?

I need your input on this project. - 이 프로젝트에 대한 당신의 의견이 필요합니다.

I need your input on this project. - 이 프로젝트에 대한 당신의 의견이 필요합니다.

The deadline for the report is approaching. - 보고서 마감일이 다가오고 있습니다.

The deadline for the report is approaching. - 보고서 마감일이 다가오고 있습니다.

Let's collaborate on this task. - 이 작업에 협력합시다.

Let's collaborate on this task. - 이 작업에 협력합시다.

I appreciate your hard work. - 당신의 노고에 감사합니다.

I appreciate your hard work. - 당신의 노고에 감사합니다.

Can you send me the agenda for the meeting? - 회의 안건을 보내주시겠어요?

Can you send me the agenda for the meeting? - 회의 안건을 보내주시겠어요?

We need to streamline our communication process. - 의사 소통 과정을 간소화해야 합니다.

We need to streamline our communication process. - 의사 소통 과정을 간소화해야 합니다.

Effective communication is essential in the workplace. - 직장에서 효과적인 의사 소통은 필수입니다.

Effective communication is essential in the workplace. - 직장에서 효과적인 의사 소통은 필수입니다.

Please keep me in the loop regarding project updates. - 프로젝트 업데이트에 대해 계속 알려주세요.

Please keep me in the loop regarding project updates. - 프로젝트 업데이트에 대해 계속 알려주세요.

I need your feedback on the proposal. - 제안에 대한 당신의 의견이 필요합니다.

I need your feedback on the proposal. - 제안에 대한 당신의 의견이 필요합니다.

Let's schedule a follow-up meeting. - 후속 회의 일정을 잡아봅시다.

Let's schedule a follow-up meeting. - 후속 회의 일정을 잡아봅시다.

We are looking for innovative solutions. - 혁신적인 해결책을 찾고 있습니다.

We are looking for innovative solutions. - 혁신적인 해결책을 찾고 있습니다.

Can you make a presentation on the latest market trends? - 최신 시장 동향에 대한 프레젠테이션을 준비할 수 있나요?

Can you make a presentation on the latest market trends? - 최신 시장 동향에 대한 프레젠테이션을 준비할 수 있나요?

Our company values teamwork and collaboration. - 우리 회사는 팀워크와 협력을 중시합니다.

Our company values teamwork and collaboration. - 우리 회사는 팀워크와 협력을 중시합니다.

It's important to set clear goals for the team. - 팀에 명확한 목표를 설정하는 것이 중요합니다.

It's important to set clear goals for the team. - 팀에 명확한 목표를 설정하는 것이 중요합니다.

We need to address the challenges in our workflow. - 워크플로우에서 발생하는 문제에 대해 대처해야 합니다.

We need to address the challenges in our workflow. - 워크플로우에서 발생하는 문제에 대해 대처해야 합니다.

Let's brainstorm ideas for the upcoming project. - 다가오는 프로젝트를 위해 아이디어를 모아봅시다.

Let's brainstorm ideas for the upcoming project. - 다가오는 프로젝트를 위해 아이디어를 모아봅시다.

We should delegate tasks efficiently. - 업무를 효율적으로 할당해야 합니다.

We should delegate tasks efficiently. - 업무를 효율적으로 할당해야 합니다.

Time management is crucial in a professional setting. - 프로페셔널한 환경에서 시간 관리는 중요합니다.

Time management is crucial in a professional setting. - 프로페셔널한 환경에서 시간 관리는 중요합니다.

I have a business trip next week. - 다음 주에 출장이 있습니다.

I have a business trip next week. - 다음 주에 출장이 있습니다.

Can you handle my responsibilities while I'm away? - 저의 책임을 부탁드릴 수 있나요?

Can you handle my responsibilities while I'm away? - 저의 책임을 부탁드릴 수 있나요?

Traveling for work can be challenging but rewarding. - 일을 위해 여행하는 것은 어렵지만 보람이 있을 수 있습니다.

Traveling for work can be challenging but rewarding. - 일을 위해 여행하는 것은 어렵지만 보람이 있을 수 있습니다.

We need to adhere to the company policies. -
회사 정책을 준수해야 합니다.

We need to adhere to the company policies. -
회사 정책을 준수해야 합니다.

Let's discuss the budget for the upcoming project.
- 다가오는 프로젝트의 예산에 대해
논의해봅시다.

Let's discuss the budget for the upcoming project.
- 다가오는 프로젝트의 예산에 대해
논의해봅시다.

Financial transparency is crucial for trust. -
신뢰를 위해 재무 투명성은 중요합니다.

Financial transparency is crucial for trust. -
신뢰를 위해 재무 투명성은 중요합니다.

Can you provide an update on the sales figures? -
판매 수치에 대한 업데이트를 제공할 수
있나요?

Can you provide an update on the sales figures? -
판매 수치에 대한 업데이트를 제공할 수
있나요?

We need to enhance our customer service. -
우리는 고객 서비스를 향상시켜야 합니다.

We need to enhance our customer service. -
우리는 고객 서비스를 향상시켜야 합니다.

Customer feedback is valuable for improvement. - 고객 피드백은 개선에 도움이 됩니다.

Customer feedback is valuable for improvement. - 고객 피드백은 개선에 도움이 됩니다.

Let's schedule a training session for the team. - 팀을 위한 교육 세션 일정을 잡아봅시다.

Let's schedule a training session for the team. - 팀을 위한 교육 세션 일정을 잡아봅시다.

Employee development is a priority for our company. - 직원 개발은 우리 회사의 우선 순위입니다.

Employee development is a priority for our company. - 직원 개발은 우리 회사의 우선 순위입니다.

I need your input on the marketing strategy. - 마케팅 전략에 대한 당신의 의견이 필요합니다.

I need your input on the marketing strategy. - 마케팅 전략에 대한 당신의 의견이 필요합니다.

Can you provide insights into market trends? - 시장 동향에 대한 통찰력을 제공할 수 있나요?

Can you provide insights into market trends? - 시장 동향에 대한 통찰력을 제공할 수 있나요?

Let's schedule a team-building activity. - 팀 빌딩
활동 일정을 잡아봅시다.

Let's schedule a team-building activity. - 팀 빌딩
활동 일정을 잡아봅시다.

Teamwork is the key to our success. - 팀워크가
우리의 성공의 열쇠입니다.

Teamwork is the key to our success. - 팀워크가
우리의 성공의 열쇠입니다.

We need to analyze the competition. - 경쟁사를
분석해야 합니다.

We need to analyze the competition. - 경쟁사를
분석해야 합니다.

What is your strategy for client acquisition? -
고객 획득을 위한 당신의 전략은
무엇인가요?

What is your strategy for client acquisition? -
고객 획득을 위한 당신의 전략은
무엇인가요?

Let's set realistic and achievable goals. -
현실적이고 달성 가능한 목표를
설정합시다.

Let's set realistic and achievable goals. -
현실적이고 달성 가능한 목표를
설정합시다.

How can we improve employee satisfaction? - 직원 만족도를 어떻게 향상시킬 수 있을까요?

How can we improve employee satisfaction? - 직원 만족도를 어떻게 향상시킬 수 있을까요?

I appreciate your dedication to the project. - 프로젝트에 대한 당신의 헌신에 감사합니다.

I appreciate your dedication to the project. - 프로젝트에 대한 당신의 헌신에 감사합니다.

Can you provide a status update on the project? - 프로젝트에 대한 상태 업데이트를 제공할 수 있나요?

Can you provide a status update on the project? - 프로젝트에 대한 상태 업데이트를 제공할 수 있나요?

Let's create a detailed project timeline. - 자세한 프로젝트 타임라인을 만들어봅시다.

Let's create a detailed project timeline. - 자세한 프로젝트 타임라인을 만들어봅시다.

We need to address any issues promptly. - 어떠한 문제도 신속하게 해결해야 합니다.

We need to address any issues promptly. - 어떠한 문제도 신속하게 해결해야 합니다.

Can you share your thoughts on the new company policy? - 새로운 회사 정책에 대한 당신의 생각을 나누어 줄 수 있나요?

Can you share your thoughts on the new company policy? - 새로운 회사 정책에 대한 당신의 생각을 나누어 줄 수 있나요?

We should conduct a performance review. - 성과 평가를 진행해야 합니다.

We should conduct a performance review. - 성과 평가를 진행해야 합니다.

Constructive feedback is essential for improvement. - 개선을 위한 건설적인 피드백이 중요합니다.

Constructive feedback is essential for improvement. - 개선을 위한 건설적인 피드백이 중요합니다.

Let's organize a team retreat for team bonding. - 팀간 유대감을 형성하기 위해 팀 소풍을 조직합시다.

Let's organize a team retreat for team bonding. - 팀간 유대감을 형성하기 위해 팀 소풍을 조직합시다.

Effective leadership is crucial for team success. - 팀의 성공을 위해서는 효과적인 리더십이 필요합니다.

Effective leadership is crucial for team success. - 팀의 성공을 위해서는 효과적인 리더십이 필요합니다.

Can we implement a flexible work schedule? - 유연한 근무 일정을 도입할 수 있을까요?

Can we implement a flexible work schedule? - 유연한 근무 일정을 도입할 수 있을까요?

Work-life balance is important for employee well-being. - 직원의 복지를 위해 업무와 일상의 균형을 맞추는 것이 중요합니다.

Work-life balance is important for employee well-being. - 직원의 복지를 위해 업무와 일상의 균형을 맞추는 것이 중요합니다.

Let's schedule a team-building workshop. - 팀 빌딩 워크샵 일정을 잡아봅시다.

Let's schedule a team-building workshop. - 팀 빌딩 워크샵 일정을 잡아봅시다.

Employee engagement is a key factor in productivity. - 직원 참여는 생산성의 핵심 요소입니다.

Employee engagement is a key factor in productivity. - 직원 참여는 생산성의 핵심 요소입니다.

We need to address the issues raised in the employee survey. - 직원 설문조사에서 제기된 문제를 해결해야 합니다.

We need to address the issues raised in the employee survey. - 직원 설문조사에서 제기된 문제를 해결해야 합니다.

Can you share your expertise with the team? - 당신의 전문 지식을 팀과 공유할 수 있을까요?

Can you share your expertise with the team? - 당신의 전문 지식을 팀과 공유할 수 있을까요?

Let's celebrate our achievements as a team. - 팀으로 성취를 축하합시다.

Let's celebrate our achievements as a team. - 팀으로 성취를 축하합시다.

What are the key performance indicators for this project? - 이 프로젝트의 주요 성과 지표는 무엇인가요?

What are the key performance indicators for this project? - 이 프로젝트의 주요 성과 지표는 무엇인가요?

Let's create a strategic plan for the next quarter. - 다음 분기를 위한 전략적인 계획을 만들어봅시다.

Let's create a strategic plan for the next quarter. - 다음 분기를 위한 전략적인 계획을 만들어봅시다.

I appreciate your attention to detail. - 세부 사항에 대한 당신의 주의에 감사합니다.

I appreciate your attention to detail. - 세부 사항에 대한 당신의 주의에 감사합니다.

Can we set up a mentorship program for junior employees? - 주니어 직원을 위한 멘토링 프로그램을 만들 수 있을까요?

Can we set up a mentorship program for junior employees? - 주니어 직원을 위한 멘토링 프로그램을 만들 수 있을까요?

Let's discuss the agenda for the upcoming board meeting. - 다가오는 이사회 회의의 안건을 논의해봅시다.

Let's discuss the agenda for the upcoming board meeting. - 다가오는 이사회 회의의 안건을 논의해봅시다.

Board members play a crucial role in decision-making. - 이사회 멤버는 결정에 중요한 역할을 합니다.

Board members play a crucial role in decision-making. - 이사회 멤버는 결정에 중요한 역할을 합니다.

Can you provide an update on the financial report? - 재무 보고서에 대한 업데이트를 제공할 수 있나요?

Can you provide an update on the financial report? - 재무 보고서에 대한 업데이트를 제공할 수 있나요?

We need to analyze the market trends before making a decision. - 결정을 내리기 전에 시장 동향을 분석해야 합니다.

We need to analyze the market trends before making a decision. - 결정을 내리기 전에 시장 동향을 분석해야 합니다.

Let's schedule a training session on data security. - 데이터 보안에 대한 교육 세션 일정을 잡아봅시다.

Let's schedule a training session on data security. - 데이터 보안에 대한 교육 세션 일정을 잡아봅시다.

Data integrity is crucial for our business operations. - 데이터 무결성은 우리 비즈니스 운영에 중요합니다.

Data integrity is crucial for our business operations. - 데이터 무결성은 우리 비즈니스 운영에 중요합니다.

Can you provide a report on the project milestones? - 프로젝트의 중간 목표에 대한 보고서를 제공할 수 있나요?

Can you provide a report on the project milestones? - 프로젝트의 중간 목표에 대한 보고서를 제공할 수 있나요?

Let's implement a feedback loop for continuous improvement. - 지속적인 개선을 위한 피드백 루프를 도입합시다.

Let's implement a feedback loop for continuous improvement. - 지속적인 개선을 위한 피드백 루프를 도입합시다.

We need to address the challenges in our supply chain. - 우리 공급망에서 발생하는 문제에 대해 대처해야 합니다.

We need to address the challenges in our supply chain. - 우리 공급망에서 발생하는 문제에 대해 대처해야 합니다.

Can you share your insights on the market competition? - 시장 경쟁에 대한 당신의 통찰력을 나누어 줄 수 있나요?

Can you share your insights on the market competition? - 시장 경쟁에 대한 당신의 통찰력을 나누어 줄 수 있나요?

Let's schedule a workshop on innovation and creativity. - 혁신과 창의성에 관한 워크샵 일정을 잡아봅시다.

Let's schedule a workshop on innovation and creativity. - 혁신과 창의성에 관한 워크샵 일정을 잡아봅시다.

Innovation is the key to staying competitive. - 혁신은 경쟁력을 유지하는 열쇠입니다.

Innovation is the key to staying competitive. - 혁신은 경쟁력을 유지하는 열쇠입니다.

Can you propose ideas for cost reduction? - 비용 감축을 위한 아이디어를 제안할 수 있나요?

Can you propose ideas for cost reduction? - 비용 감축을 위한 아이디어를 제안할 수 있나요?

Navigating the City:

Where is the subway station? - 지하철역 어디에요? (Jihacheol-yeog eodi-e-yo?)

Where is the subway station? - 지하철역 어디에요? (Jihacheol-yeog eodi-e-yo?)

How do I get to [place]? - [장소]로 가려면 어떻게 가야 해요? ([Jangso]-ro galyeomyeon eotteohge gaya haeyo?)

How do I get to [place]? - [장소]로 가려면 어떻게 가야 해요? ([Jangso]-ro galyeomyeon eotteohge gaya haeyo?)

Is it far from here? - 여기서 멀어요? (Yeogiseo meol-eoyo?)

Is it far from here? - 여기서 멀어요? (Yeogiseo meol-eoyo?)

Can you show me on the map? - 지도로 보여주실 수 있나요? (Jido-ro boyeojusil su issnayo?)

Can you show me on the map? - 지도로 보여주실 수 있나요? (Jido-ro boyeojusil su issnayo?)

Which bus goes to [destination]? - [목적지]로 가는 버스 어디에요? ([Mokjeokji]-ro ganeun beoseu eodi-e-yo?)

Which bus goes to [destination]? - [목적지]로 가는 버스 어디에요? ([Mokjeokji]-ro ganeun beoseu eodi-e-yo?)

How much is a ticket to [destination]? - [목적지] 가는 표 얼마에요? ([Mokjeokji] ganeun pyo eolmae-yo?)

How much is a ticket to [destination]? - [목적지] 가는 표 얼마에요? ([Mokjeokji] ganeun pyo eolmae-yo?)

Is there a taxi stand nearby? - 근처에 택시 승강장이 있나요? (Geuncheo-e taeksi seunggangjang-i issnayo?)

Is there a taxi stand nearby? - 근처에 택시 승강장이 있나요? (Geuncheo-e taeksi seunggangjang-i issnayo?)

I need a taxi. - 택시가 필요해요. (Taeksi-ga pil-yo-haeyo.)

I need a taxi. - 택시가 필요해요. (Taeksi-ga pil-yo-haeyo.)

What's the fastest way to get there? - 가장 빠른 길은 뭐에요? (Gajang bbal-eun gil-eun mwoeyo?)

What's the fastest way to get there? - 가장 빠른 길은 뭐에요? (Gajang bbal-eun gil-eun mwoeyo?)

Can you recommend a scenic route? - 경치 좋은 길을 추천해 주세요. (Gyeongchi joeun gil-eul chucheonhae juseyo.)

Can you recommend a scenic route? - 경치 좋은 길을 추천해 주세요. (Gyeongchi joeun gil-eul chucheonhae juseyo.)

What time does the next bus/train arrive? - 다음 버스/기차는 몇 시에 도착해요? (Daeum beoseu/gicha-neun myeot shi-e dochakhaeyo?)

What time does the next bus/train arrive? - 다음 버스/기차는 몇 시에 도착해요? (Daeum beoseu/gicha-neun myeot shi-e dochakhaeyo?)

How often do buses/trains run? - 버스/기차는 얼마나 자주 다녀요? (Beoseu/gicha-neun eolmana jaju danyeoyo?)

How often do buses/trains run? - 버스/기차는 얼마나 자주 다녀요? (Beoseu/gicha-neun eolmana jaju danyeoyo?)

Which subway line is this? - 이 지하철은 몇 호선이에요? (I jihacheol-eun myeot hoseon-i-e-yo?)

Which subway line is this? - 이 지하철은 몇 호선이에요? (I jihacheol-eun myeot hoseon-i-e-yo?)

Do I need to transfer? - 환승해야 돼요? (Hwanseung-haeya dwaeyo?)

Do I need to transfer? - 환승해야 돼요? (Hwanseung-haeya dwaeyo?)

Is this the right platform for [destination]? - 이게 [목적지]로 가는 플랫폼 맞아요? (Ige [Mokjeokji]-ro ganeun peullaetpom majayo?)

Is this the right platform for [destination]? - 이게 [목적지]로 가는 플랫폼 맞아요? (Ige [Mokjeokji]-ro ganeun peullaetpom majayo?)

How many stops to [destination]? - [목적지]까지 몇 정거장이에요? ([Mokjeokji]-kkaji myeot jeong-geo-jang-i-e-yo?)

How many stops to [destination]? - [목적지]까지 몇 정거장이에요? ([Mokjeokji]-kkaji myeot jeong-geo-jang-i-e-yo?)

Where is the bus stop? - 버스 정류장 어디에요? (Beoseu jeonglyujang eodi-e-yo?)

Where is the bus stop? - 버스 정류장 어디에요? (Beoseu jeonglyujang eodi-e-yo?)

What's the last stop on this route? - 이 노선의 종착역은 어디에요? (I noseon-ui jongchag-yeog-eun eodi-e-yo?)

What's the last stop on this route? - 이 노선의 종착역은 어디에요? (I noseon-ui jongchag-yeog-eun eodi-e-yo?)

How much is a one-way ticket? - 편도 표 얼마에요? (Pyendo pyo eolmae-yo?)

How much is a one-way ticket? - 편도 표 얼마에요? (Pyendo pyo eolmae-yo?)

Is there a discount for students/seniors? - 학생/노인 할인이 있나요? (Hagsaeng/no-in haling-i issnayo?)

Is there a discount for students/seniors? - 학생/노인 할인이 있나요? (Hagsaeng/no-in haling-i issnayo?)

Excuse me, where is [landmark]? - 실례합니다, [랜드마크] 어디에요? (Sillyehamnida, [Laendeumakeu] eodi-e-yo?)

Excuse me, where is [landmark]? - 실례합니다, [랜드마크] 어디에요? (Sillyehamnida, [Laendeumakeu] eodi-e-yo?)

Can you tell me how to get to the nearest bank? - 가장 가까운 은행 가는 길 좀 알려주세요. (Gajang gakkawoon eunhaeng ganeun gil jom allyeojuseyo.)

Can you tell me how to get to the nearest bank? - 가장 가까운 은행 가는 길 좀 알려주세요. (Gajang gakkawoon eunhaeng ganeun gil jom allyeojuseyo.)

I'm looking for the post office. - 우체국을 찾고 있어요. (Ucheguk-eul chajgo iss-eoyo.)

I'm looking for the post office. - 우체국을 찾고 있어요. (Ucheguk-eul chajgo iss-eoyo.)

Which way is [street name]? - [거리 이름] 어디에요? ([Geoli ileum] eodi-e-yo?)

Which way is [street name]? - [거리 이름] 어디에요? ([Geoli ileum] eodi-e-yo?)

Is [place] within walking distance? - [장소] 걸어서 갈 수 있을까요? ([Jangso] geoleo-seo gal su iss-eulkka yo?)

Is [place] within walking distance? - [장소] 걸어서 갈 수 있을까요? ([Jangso] geoleo-seo gal su iss-eulkka yo?)

Can you show me the way on my phone map? - 핸드폰 지도로 길을 보여주실 수 있나요? (Haendeupon jido-lo gil-eul boyeojusil su issnayo?)

Can you show me the way on my phone map? - 핸드폰 지도로 길을 보여주실 수 있나요? (Haendeupon jido-lo gil-eul boyeojusil su issnayo?)

Is there a shortcut to [destination]? - [목적지]로 가는 지름길이 있나요? ([Mokjeokji]-ro ganeun jileum-gil-i issnayo?)

Is there a shortcut to [destination]? - [목적지]로 가는 지름길이 있나요? ([Mokjeokji]-ro ganeun jileum-gil-i issnayo?)

How far is it to the nearest ATM? - 가장 가까운 ATM까지 얼마나 멀어요? (Gajang gakkawoon

ATM-kkaji eolmana meol-eoyo?)How far is it to the nearest ATM? - 가장 가까운 ATM까지 얼마나 멀어요? (Gajang gakkawoon ATM-kkaji eolmana meol-eoyo?)

I'm lost. Can you help me find my way? - 길을 잃었어요. 제 방향 찾는 데 도와주세요. (Gileul ilh-eosseoyo. Je banghyang chajneun de dowajuseyo.)

I'm lost. Can you help me find my way? - 길을 잃었어요. 제 방향 찾는 데 도와주세요. (Gileul ilh-eosseoyo. Je banghyang chajneun de dowajuseyo.)

Excuse me, is this the right road to [destination]? - 실례합니다, 이게 [목적지]로 가는 길이 맞아요? (Sillyehamnida, Ige [Mokjeokji]-ro ganeun gil-i majayo?)

Excuse me, is this the right road to [destination]? - 실례합니다, 이게 [목적지]로 가는 길이 맞아요? (Sillyehamnida, Ige [Mokjeokji]-ro ganeun gil-i majayo?)

What's the address here? - 여기 주소가 뭐에요? (Yeogi juso-ga mwoeyo?)

What's the address here? - 여기 주소가 뭐에요? (Yeogi juso-ga mwoeyo?)

Are there any public restrooms nearby? - 근처에 화장실이 있나요? (Geuncheo-e hwajangsil-i issnayo?)

Are there any public restrooms nearby? - 근처에 화장실이 있나요? (Geuncheo-e hwajangsil-i issnayo?)

Can you recommend a good local cafe? - 좋은 현지 카페 추천해 주시겠어요? (Joeun hyeonji kape chucheonhae jushigess-eoyo?)Can you recommend a good local cafe? - 좋은 현지 카페 추천해 주시겠어요? (Joeun hyeonji kape chucheonhae jushigess-eoyo?)

How late is this place open? - 여기는 몇 시까지 열어있어요? (Yeogineun myeot shi-kkaji yeol-eoiss-eoyo?)

How late is this place open? - 여기는 몇 시까지 열어있어요? (Yeogineun myeot shi-kkaji yeol-eoiss-eoyo?)

Where can I buy a SIM card for my phone? - 핸드폰용 SIM 카드는 어디서 살 수 있어요? (Haendeupon-yong SIM kadeu-neun eodiseo sal su iss-eoyo?)

Where can I buy a SIM card for my phone? - 핸드폰용 SIM 카드는 어디서 살 수 있어요? (Haendeupon-yong SIM kadeu-neun eodiseo sal su iss-eoyo?)

Can you recommend a good spot for sightseeing? - 볼만한 곳을 추천해 주실래요? (Bolmanhan goseul chucheonhae juseulraeyo?)

Can you recommend a good spot for sightseeing? - 볼만한 곳을 추천해 주실래요? (Bolmanhan goseul chucheonhae juseulraeyo?)

Is there a tourist information center around here? - 여기 근처에 관광 안내소가 있나요? (Yeogi geuncheo-e gwangwang annaesoga issnayo?)

Is there a tourist information center around here? - 여기 근처에 관광 안내소가 있나요? (Yeogi geuncheo-e gwangwang annaesoga issnayo?)

I'd like to rent a bicycle. - 자전거 빌리고 싶어요. (Jajeongeo billigo sip-eoyo.)

I'd like to rent a bicycle. - 자전거 빌리고 싶어요. (Jajeongeo billigo sip-eoyo.)

What's the best way to get to the airport? - 공항으로 가는 가장 좋은 방법이 뭐에요? (Gonghang-eulo ganeun gajang joeun bangbeob-i mwoeyo?)

What's the best way to get to the airport? - 공항으로 가는 가장 좋은 방법이 뭐에요? (Gonghang-eulo ganeun gajang joeun bangbeob-i mwoeyo?)

Can you recommend a good local market? - 좋은 현지 시장 추천해 주시겠어요? (Joeun hyeonji sijang chucheonhae jushigess-eoyo?)

Can you recommend a good local market? - 좋은 현지 시장 추천해 주시겠어요? (Joeun hyeonji sijang chucheonhae jushigess-eoyo?)

Romantic Phrases

I love you. - 사랑해.

I love you. - 사랑해.

You mean the world to me. - 넌 나에게 세상을 의미해.

You mean the world to me. - 넌 나에게 세상을 의미해.

You are my everything. - 넌 나의 전부야.

You are my everything. - 넌 나의 전부야.

I adore you. - 나는 너를 숭배해.

I adore you. - 나는 너를 숭배해.

You complete me. - 너는 나를 완성시켜.

You complete me. - 너는 나를 완성시켜.

You make my heart race. - 너는 나의 심장을 뛰게 해.

You make my heart race. - 너는 나의 심장을 뛰게 해.

I can't live without you. - 너 없이는 살 수 없어.

I can't live without you. - 너 없이는 살 수 없어.

You're the love of my life. - 넌 나의 인생의 사랑이야.

You're the love of my life. - 넌 나의 인생의 사랑이야.

I cherish every moment with you. - 너와 함께한 모든 순간을 소중히 여겨.

I cherish every moment with you. - 너와 함께한 모든 순간을 소중히 여겨.

My heart belongs to you. - 나의 마음은 네게 속해있어.

My heart belongs to you. - 나의 마음은 네게 속해있어.

You're my soulmate. - 넌 나의 소울메이트야.

You're my soulmate. - 넌 나의 소울메이트야.

I'm grateful to have you in my life. - 나는 너를 내 삶에 두어 고맙다.

I'm grateful to have you in my life. - 나는 너를 내 삶에 두어 고맙다.

I miss you. - 보고 싶어.

I miss you. - 보고 싶어.

I think about you all the time. - 항상 당신을 생각해.

I think about you all the time. - 항상 당신을 생각해.

You're always on my mind. - 넌 항상 내 마음속에 있어.

You're always on my mind. - 넌 항상 내 마음속에 있어.

You're the one for me. - 넌 나에게 딱 맞는 사람이야.

You're the one for me. - 넌 나에게 딱 맞는 사람이야.

I'm lucky to have you. - 나는 널 가질 수 있어 행운이야.

I'm lucky to have you. - 나는 널 가질 수 있어 행운이야.

You're my happiness. - 넌 나의 행복이야.

You're my happiness. - 넌 나의 행복이야.

You're my sunshine. - 넌 나의 햇살이야.

You're my sunshine. - 넌 나의 햇살이야.

I'm crazy about you. - 나는 너에게 미쳐가.

I'm crazy about you. - 나는 너에게 미쳐가.

You're the most beautiful person I've ever met. - 넌 나가 만난 가장 아름다운 사람이야.

You're the most beautiful person I've ever met. - 넌 나가 만난 가장 아름다운 사람이야.

I can't resist your charm. - 나는 네 매력에 저항할 수 없어.

I can't resist your charm. - 나는 네 매력에 저항할 수 없어.

I love your smile. - 네 웃음을 사랑해.

I love your smile. - 네 웃음을 사랑해.

You make my world brighter. - 너는 나의 세계를 더 밝게 만들어.

You make my world brighter. - 너는 나의 세계를 더 밝게 만들어.

You're the love story I've always dreamed of. - 넌 나가 항상 꿈꾸던 사랑 이야기야.

You're the love story I've always dreamed of. - 넌 나가 항상 꿈꾸던 사랑 이야기야.

My love for you is endless. - 나의 너에 대한 사랑은 끝없어.

My love for you is endless. - 나의 너에 대한 사랑은 끝없어.

You're my one and only. - 넌 나의 유일한 사랑이야.

You're my one and only. - 넌 나의 유일한 사랑이야.

You're my dream come true. - 넌 나의 꿈이 현실이 된 것이야.

You're my dream come true. - 넌 나의 꿈이 현실이 된 것이야.

You're the reason I believe in love. - 넌 나가 사랑을 믿게 해준 이유야.

You're the reason I believe in love. - 넌 나가 사랑을 믿게 해준 이유야.

Every moment with you is precious. - 너와 함께한 모든 순간은 소중해.

Every moment with you is precious. - 너와 함께한 모든 순간은 소중해.

You're my heart's desire. - 넌 나의 마음의 소망이야.

You're my heart's desire. - 넌 나의 마음의 소망이야.

I want to grow old with you. - 나는 너와 함께 나이를 먹고 싶어.

I want to grow old with you. - 나는 너와 함께 나이를 먹고 싶어.

Your love is a treasure. - 너의 사랑은 보물이야.

Your love is a treasure. - 너의 사랑은 보물이야.

I'm enchanted by your kindness. - 나는 네 친절에 마법처럼 사로잡혀.

I'm enchanted by your kindness. - 나는 네 친절에 마법처럼 사로잡혀.

You're the melody of my life. - 넌 나의 인생의 멜로디야.

You're the melody of my life. - 넌 나의 인생의 멜로디야.

I love the way you look at me. - 나는 네가 나를 바라보는 방식을 사랑해.

I love the way you look at me. - 나는 네가 나를 바라보는 방식을 사랑해.

You're my refuge in the storm. - 넌 폭풍 속에서 나의 피난처야.

You're my refuge in the storm. - 넌 폭풍 속에서 나의 피난처야.

Your touch is electric. - 네 손길은 전기처럼 느껴져.

Your touch is electric. - 네 손길은 전기처럼 느껴져.

You're my greatest adventure. - 넌 나의 최고의 모험이야.

You're my greatest adventure. - 넌 나의 최고의 모험이야.

I am devoted to you. - 나는 네게 헌신되어 있다.

I am devoted to you. - 나는 네게 헌신되어 있다.

You're the one who completes me. - 넌 나를 완성시켜주는 사람이야.

You're the one who completes me. - 넌 나를 완성시켜주는 사람이야.

I love the way you make me feel. - 나는 네가 나에게 느끼게 하는 감정을 사랑해.

I love the way you make me feel. - 나는 네가 나에게 느끼게 하는 감정을 사랑해.

You're the fire in my soul. - 넌 나의 영혼 속의 불꽃이야.

You're the fire in my soul. - 넌 나의 영혼 속의 불꽃이야.

Our love is like a fairytale. - 우리의 사랑은 동화같아.

Our love is like a fairytale. - 우리의 사랑은 동화같아.

I am endlessly grateful for you. - 나는 너에게 끝없이 감사하다.

I am endlessly grateful for you. - 나는 너에게 끝없이 감사하다.

You're my muse. - 넌 나의 영감이야.

You're my muse. - 넌 나의 영감이야.

I want to make you happy. - 나는 너를 행복하게 하고 싶어.

I want to make you happy. - 나는 너를 행복하게 하고 싶어.

Your laughter is my favorite sound. - 네 웃음은 나의 가장 좋아하는 소리야.

Your laughter is my favorite sound. - 네 웃음은 나의 가장 좋아하는 소리야.

You're the one I've been searching for. - 넌 나가 찾고 있던 사람이야.

You're the one I've been searching for. - 넌 나가 찾고 있던 사람이야.

Our love is a journey with no end. - 우리의 사랑은 끝이 없는 여정이야.

Our love is a journey with no end. - 우리의 사랑은 끝이 없는 여정이야.

Conclusion

In conclusion, mastering the essentials of the Korean language opens a gateway to a rich cultural experience and seamless communication in various contexts. This phrasebook serves as a valuable companion, offering not only linguistic insights but also a bridge to deeper cultural understanding. Whether navigating bustling markets, engaging in heartfelt conversations, or exploring the captivating landscapes of Korea, the phrases within these pages empower you to connect authentically with locals and immerse yourself in the vibrant tapestry of Korean life. As you embark on your language journey, remember that language is not merely a tool for communication but a key to unlocking the warmth and hospitality of a community. Embrace the adventure of learning Korean, and may the phrases within these pages enhance your travels, foster meaningful connections, and enrich your overall experience in the beautiful land of Korea. Safe travels, or as they say in Korean, 안녕히 가세요 (annyeonghi gaseyo)!